Catering and Hospitality
NVQ/SVQ 2

Food Preparation and Cooking: Core Units

Student Guide

SECOND EDITION

Ann Bulleid, Philip Coulthard,
Rowland Foote, David Klaasen,
Pam Rabone, Malcolm Ware

First published in 1993 by:
Stanley Thornes (Publishers) Ltd
Second edition 1996

Reprinted in 2001 by:
Nelson Thornes Ltd
Delta Place
27 Bath Road
CHELTENHAM
GL53 7TH
United Kingdom

        05 06 / 15 14 13 12 11 10

A catalogue record for this book is available from the British Library

ISBN 0 7487 2567 9

Illustrations by Linda Herd
Page make-up by Columns Design Ltd

Printed in Great Britain by Scotprint

Contents

Acknowledgements

The authors and publishers would like to thank Andy Armiger, Bill Moorcroft, Andy Robertson and Tony Groves for their help and advice. They would also like to thank the following for permission to reproduce photographs: Lockhart Catering Equipment (pp. 5, 48 (bottom), 50, 52, 54, 92), Lever Industrial (p. 48 (top)), Rowland Foote (pp. 66, 67, 68, 69, 72, 73, 74, 75, 76, 77, 78, 80, 81, 84, 85), Andrew Nisbet and Co Ltd (pp. 61, 62), Digital Stock (cover photograph).

Maintain a safe and secure working environment

This chapter covers:

ELEMENT 1: **Maintain personal health and hygiene**
ELEMENT 2: **Carry out procedures in the event of a fire**
ELEMENT 3: **Maintain a safe environment for customers, staff and visitors**
ELEMENT 4: **Maintain a secure environment for customers, staff and visitors**

What you need to do

- Carry out your work in line with hygiene practices
- Take account of customers', staff and visitors' reactions when involved with emergencies and deal with them accordingly.
- Identify hazards or potential hazards and take appropriate action to deal with the situation.
- Take precautionary measures to warn customers, staff and visitors of hazards or potential hazards.
- Identify all company procedures for dealing with emergency situations.
- Comply with all relevant health and safety legislation.
- Ensure that safety and security procedures and practices are followed at all times in a calm, orderly manner.
- Work in an organised and efficient manner in line with appropriate organisational procedures and legal requirements.

What you need to know

- Why it is important to comply with health and safety legislation.
- Where and from whom information on health and safety legislation can be obtained.
- Why preventative action must always be taken quickly when a potential hazard is spotted.
- What action to take when dealing with an emergency situation such as fire, accident or the discovery of a suspicious item or package.
- Who to contact in the event of an emergency and the information they will need.
- How to identify and deal with safety hazards or potential safety hazards for customers, staff and visitors.
- Why suspicious items or packages should never be approached or tampered with.
- Why suspicious items or packages must always be reported immediately.
- The procedures for ensuring the security of the establishment and property within it.
- Why keys, property and storage areas should be secured from unauthorised access at all times.
- What action to take when challenging suspicious individuals.
- What action to take when establishment, customer or staff property is reported missing.

ELEMENT 1:   Maintain personal health and hygiene

INTRODUCTION

The image you project while dealing with customers can say a great deal about the way your company operates. People are more likely to use a restaurant or food outlet if they can see that the staff take care of their appearance and follow good hygiene practices when dealing with food.

As well as looking good, everyone involved in the preparation and service of food has a duty under the Food Hygiene Regulations to protect food from risk of contamination by careful storage and handling. You will find this covered in more detail in Units 1ND1 and 2ND11. In food areas in particular there are legal requirements which influence all aspects of the way we work.

FOOD HYGIENE REGULATIONS

The Food Hygiene Regulations, particularly those related to food handlers, identify and lay down the legal requirements for the main risk areas and included them in the appropriate legislation known as *Food Hygiene (General) Regulations 1970*.

This legislation has been amended and updated by the *Food Safety Act 1990* which is now the main 'enabling act' under which any future regulations will be passed. The features contained within the 1970 regulations are retained within this new Act and have been amended, where necessary, to reflect the tighter regulations contained within the new act.

The new Food Safety Act came about as a response to genuine public concern about the risks associated with food preparation and production and the increase in the numbers of incidents of food related illnesses.

The Food Safety Act has been developed to take account and to impact on every stage of the food chain from its source to its presentation and consumption by the customer. This means there needs to be even more care and attention when dealing with the service of food and drink. The Act has increased the scope and impact of penalties and includes, in brief, the following main provisions:
● includes an offence of supplying food that fails to comply with food safety requirements
● strengthens powers of enforcement, including detention and seizure of food
● requires training in basic food hygiene for all food handlers
● requires registration of all food premises
● enables Environmental Health Officers to issue emergency Prohibition Notices to force caterers to stop using the food premises or equipment immediately.

> **MEMORY JOGGER**
>
> What are the main provisions of the Food Safety Act 1990?

Complying with legislation

The impact on an establishment if they contravene hygiene regulations can be significant and could lead to a loss or even closure of the business. As an employee working within an establishment, you have a responsibility to comply with the regulations, to carry out your work to the standards expected and to ensure you attend any training in basic food handling you are required to.

The Environmental Health Officers (EHOs) are responsible for enforcing the regulations and have a number of powers which include:
1 being able to enter food premises to investigate possible offences
2 inspecting food and where necessary detaining suspect food or seizing it to be condemned
3 asking for information and gaining assistance.

An EHO also has the power to issue Improvement Notices if they feel there is a potential risk to the public. They may also, where it is felt there has been a breach of the legislation, impose a Prohibition Order which closes all or part of the premises.

The Food Safety Act has increased the maximum penalties available to the courts and these include:
- up to two years imprisonment for offenders or the imposition of unlimited fines (in Crown Courts)
- up to £2,000 per offence and a prison sentence of up to six months (through a Magistrates Court) – up to a maximum of £20,000.

There are also penalties for obstructing an Enforcement Officer.

Complying with the legislation is important as the fines may not just relate to an employer, but can also effect an employee who contravenes the legislation and fails to demonstrate hygienic working practices.

Finding out about current legislation

When you are working in an establishment you should be able to find out about the Food Hygiene legislation through your manager or supervisor. There should be information and copies of the legislation available on the premises in which you work, so it is important you find out where this is kept and make use of it. You will also find out further information through the training sessions your manager or supervisor will organise for you.

The library is also a good source of information on this subject, as well as keeping up to date through Trade Magazines, newspapers etc. You will also find the local Environmental Health Office will be able to supply information should you need it.

Do this

- Find out where the establishment displays Food Hygiene information.
- Look out for new hygiene information related to your work in magazines and newspapers.

Your responsibilities under the hygiene regulations:

As a food handler, you need to be aware of the ways in which your clothes, habits and attention to personal cleanliness can increase or reduce the risk of food contamination.

Under the *Food Hygiene (General) Regulations 1970* the food handler's responsibilities are clearly stated.

Food handlers must:
1. protect food from risk of infection
2. wear suitable protective clothing
3. wash hands after visiting the toilet
4. not smoke, spit or take snuff in food rooms
5. cover cuts or wounds with clean washable dressing
6. report illness or contact with illness.

Much of the guidance given to food handlers is aimed at reducing the risk of bacterial food poisoning. This is achieved by:
1. protecting the food from contamination through people by the wearing of protective clothing
2. ensuring that everyone is aware of the main sources of bacteria, i.e. the throat, hair, bowels and hands
3. ensuring that everyone follows basic guidelines on personal hygiene.

The number of reported cases of food poisoning has been increasing in recent years and many of the outbreaks can be traced back to contamination passing from people to food.

SOURCES OF FOOD POISONING

If you are involved in food handling it is important to be aware of the most common sources of infection so that you can take practical measures to prevent food poisoning outbreaks.

There are three main sources of food poisoning:
1 *natural sources*, such as poisonous plants (eg. toadstools, deadly nightshade). People who eat these plants are likely to develop food poisoning because of the natural poison contained in the plants
2 *chemical or metal contamination*, such as pesticides, cleaning fluids, mercury, lead or copper. Food poisoning from this source can be caused through the chemical being inadvertently spilt into the food
3 *bacteria* and germs, such as salmonella, staphylococcus, clostridium perfringens. These are naturally present all around us and can easily contaminate food if we do not follow good personal hygiene practices. Bacteria are microscopic and invisible to the naked eye, so it is difficult to know when you may be carrying bacteria which can cause food poisoning. Bacteria such as staphylococcus are naturally found on the human body, particularly in the ears, nose, throat and on the hands. Other bacteria can be carried in the intestines and can contaminate food through poor personal hygiene, e.g. forgetting to wash hands after using the toilet. Some bacteria, such as salmonella, can be transferred from one source to another through clothes, dirty hands and knives.

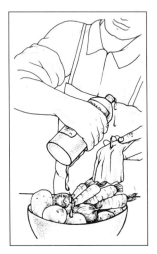

Chemical contamination can occur through accidents in the kitchen

Personal hygiene

In order to reduce the risk of infecting or cross-contaminating food, it is essential for food handlers to observe basic principles of personal hygiene. Most of these principles are common sense and have a place in our daily life, but they need to be emphasised to ensure we comply with our responsibilities under the Food Hygiene Regulations and minimise the risks to ourselves and others.

All of the points listed below are essential parts of good hygiene practice.

Keep your hands clean
Wash hands as often as necessary, but particularly:
● before starting work
● before handling food
● when moving between jobs
● after visiting the toilet
● after touching your nose, hair or ears
● after smoking.

Washing your hands regularly prevents germs from contaminating food

Bacteria on the hands can be one of the main methods of spreading infection. It may be that you have visited the toilet and have bacteria on your hands which can easily be spread if you were to return straight to work without washing them.

Finishing one job, such as boning chicken, and then moving on to, for example, mixing mayonnaise may also result in you transferring salmonella bacteria from the chicken to the mayonnaise.

Use disposable tissues in food areas
Germs are present in your ear, nose and throat. It is very easy to transfer bacteria by sneezing without using a tissue, or by spitting or picking your ears or nose, and you should *never* do this. If you need to use a tissue, use a disposable one and wash your hands immediately afterwards.

The water flow for this wash basin is controlled by a knee-operated facility, preventing the hand contact which can cause cross-contamination.

Keep fingernails short, free from nail polish and use a nail brush to clean them
Bacteria can gather under nails and spread when your hands touch food. It is a legal requirement that all wash hand basins in food preparation areas are equipped with soap, nailbrushes and disposable paper towels or blow dryers.

Avoid wearing nail polish, even if uncoloured, as it can chip and fall into food, contaminating it.

Wear only plain rings
Ornate jewellery can harbour bacteria and cause infection. Food particles may also damage the stones, or cause them to fall out. Rings can also be a safety hazard as they can become hot and burn you, or become trapped in machinery.

Keep hair away from food
Food becomes very unappetising if a stray hair has been allowed to fall into it. Hair will carry germs and can infect the food.

The Food Hygiene Regulations require you to:
● wear head covering to reduce the risk of loose hairs falling into food
● keep hair clean by regular washing. This will reduce the risk of bacteria accumulating on hair and may improve general appearance
● keep hair, moustaches and beards neat and tidy. This will reduce risks from bacteria carried on hair
● never comb hair anywhere near food.

GENERAL HEALTH AND PERSONAL HYGIENE

Food handlers should be in good general health. The guidelines given below will help to ensure this.
1 Do not work if you have any symptoms linked to food poisoning or have been in contact with someone who has, for example: vomiting, diarrhoea, stomach pains and infections. Report your symptoms to your supervisor. Your kitchen will display a staff notice reminding you to do this.
2 Wash and shower daily to reduce body odour and risks from bacteria. Wear deodorant to reduce the possibility of offensive odours.
3 Cover any cuts or bruises with a clean waterproof dressing. The dressing should be coloured blue so that it can not be 'lost' in food.
4 Avoid working with food if you have any infected and/or unsightly wounds which are likely to cause danger to customers.
5 Avoid bad habits such as:
   ● licking fingers when opening bags or picking up paper
   ● picking, scratching or touching your nose
   ● scratching your head or spots

MEMORY JOGGER

What should food handlers do when working with food to ensure they comply with the Food Hygiene Regulations?

- tasting food with an unwashed spoon
- dipping your fingers into food
- coughing or sneezing over food
- smoking
- using wash hand basins for washing food or utensils.

All of these habits can cause bacteria to spread and *must be avoided at all times*. These habits are also unpleasant to watch and may be off-putting to your customers and colleagues.

Staff Sickness Notice

If you develop any illness involving vomiting or diarrhoea, or have come into contact with anyone with these symptoms, you must report it to your Department Manager before commencing work.

Other illnesses you must report to your Manager include: abdominal pain, skin rashes, fever, septic skin, lesions or discharges from your ear, nose or throat.

The Food Hygiene Act requires you to report any sickness

Essential knowledge	Illness and infections should always be reported immediately, In order to: ● avoid spreading the disease to other staff ● avoid contamination of food ● allow action to be taken in alerting appropriate people.

Case study	*One day, when you are working a lunch shift in the kitchen you notice a colleague has been quieter than usual and seems a little under the weather. He has been preparing lunch as usual but has mentioned to you he has been feeling sick and has had a bout of diarrhoea.* *1 What is the potential risk to your customers in this situation?* *2 What would you advise your colleague to do?* *3 What action would you take in this situation?*

PROTECTIVE CLOTHING

Protective clothing is specified and required to be worn under the Food Hygiene Regulations. Many companies provide clothing for their staff and it is often the employees' responsibility to ensure they wear the correct clothing and keep it clean and in good repair.

The following guidelines are essential basic practices:
- *wear protective clothing* when in a food preparation area. This helps prevent the risk of transmitting bacteria from your non-work clothing to food. Everyday clothing can easily be contaminated by contact with pets, soil and other people
- *do not wear protective clothing outside food areas*, eg. to travel to and from work, as this can eliminate its effectiveness
- *keep your protective clothing in good condition*, without tears or missing buttons. Damaged protective clothing can look unsightly and become dangerous if you catch it on machinery, pan handles, edges of worktops, etc.

MEMORY JOGGER

Why is it important to ensure food handlers are wearing the correct protective clothing, footwear and headgear?

● *keep your clothing clean and change it daily*. The clothing should be light coloured and washable as food stains and dirt harbour bacteria. Avoid using aprons and kitchen cloths for hand drying as this can lead to cross-contamination

● *keep outdoor footwear separate* from indoor to reduce risks of infection. Alternate the shoes you wear, both to ensure foot odour is kept to a minimum and to protect your feet

● *do not wear worn or open shoes*, as these will not give you adequate protection if a spillage occurs or an article (such as a knife) is dropped onto your feet. Open shoes also offer little support if you happen to slip on a wet floor. Low-heeled, closed shoes give you the most protection and help you move quickly and efficiently about your place of work

● *wear clean socks, flesh-coloured stockings or tights* to maintain a professional and hygienic appearance.

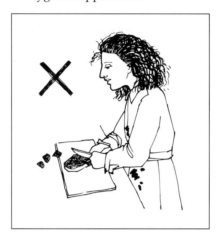 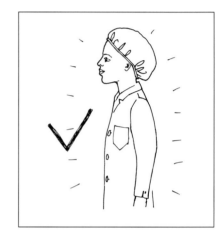

Wear clean, protective clothing

General appearance

● Avoid wearing too much make-up or perfume as it may seem unpleasant to customers. Strong perfume or aftershave can be transferred to glasses and crockery tainting the food or drink you may be handling.

● Do not carry excess items in your pockets, such as pens, tissues or money as this can look untidy and unprofessional.

Essential knowledge	Correct clothing, footwear and headgear should be worn at all times in order to: ● maintain a clean and professional appearance ● avoid the risk of contamination of food from hair and bacteria ● ensure personal freshness and eliminate the risk of body odour ● prevent accidents, i.e. through clothes or jewellery coming into contact with machinery ● ensure comfort during work periods.

HYGIENE CHECKLIST

Follow good personal hygiene practice:
● wash your hair and body regularly
● wear clean protective clothing
● wear protective hair covering and keep your hair tidy
● wash hands after visiting the toilet, touching your hair or face, smoking or preparing food
● use clean utensils and equipment at all times

- use only disposable tissues and towels or hand dryers
- report any illness or contact with ill people to your supervisor immediately
- keep all cuts and wounds covered with a clean waterproof dressing.

Do this

- Examine the uniform or protective clothing you wear and check it is clean and in good repair.
- Check yourself against the points listed above to see if you comply with personal hygiene requirements.
- Check that *Wash hands* notices are prominently displayed in wash areas, near wash hand basins and in toilet areas.
- Carry out spot checks to ensure that the wash basins are being used for handwashing only and are supplied with soap, towels and a nail brush.

What have you learned

1 Why is it important to comply with H&S legislation?
2 Why is it important to wear the correct clothing, footwear and headgear?
3 Which parts of the body can harbour harmful bacteria?
4 When should you wash your hands?
5 Why should illness and infections always be reported?
6 Which areas of the body need to be protected?
7 Give five examples of good personal hygiene practice you must follow at work.
8 Where can you obtain information on current health and safety legislation?

ELEMENT 2:   Carry out procedures in the event of a fire

INTRODUCTION

Fires occur each week on premises where staff are working and customers or visitors are present. Many, fortunately, are quite small and can be dealt with quickly. Others lead to tragic loss of life, personal injury and devastation of property.

Some of these fires could have been prevented with a little forethought, care and organisation. The commonest causes are misuse of electrical or heating equipment, and carelessly discarded cigarette-ends. People are often the link needed to start a fire: by acting negligently, perhaps by leaving rubbish in a dark corner, or by being lazy and taking shortcuts in work methods.

Fire legislation

The Fire Precautions Act 1971 requires companies to comply with certain legal conditions, such as those listed below.
- providing a suitable means of escape, which is unlocked, unobstructed, working and available whenever people are in the building
- ensuring suitable fire fighting equipment is properly maintained and readily available
- meeting the necessary requirements for a fire certificate
- posting relevent emergency signs around the area giving people guidance on what to do in the event of a fire and where to go.

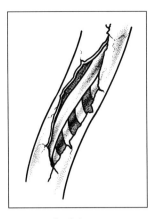

Damaged wiring

MEMORY JOGGER

What are the main causes of fire in the working environment?

MEMORY JOGGER

What can employees do in their daily work to help prevent a fire breaking out?

Causes of fire

Fire can break out wherever there is a combination of fuel, heat and oxygen. As part of your responsibility in ensuring the safety of yourself, colleagues and customers you need to be aware of some of the most common causes of fire. These are:

- *rubbish*. Fires love rubbish. Accumulations of cartons, packing materials and other combustible waste products are all potential flashpoints
- *electricity*. Although you cannot see it, the current running through your electric wiring is a source of heat and, if a fault develops in the wiring, that heat can easily become excessive and start a fire. Neglect and misuse of wiring and electrical appliances are the leading causes of fires in business premises
- *smoking*. The discarded cigarette-end is still one of the most frequent fire starters. Disposing of waste correctly will help reduce fires from this source, but even so, remember that wherever cigarettes and matches are used there is a chance of a fire starting
- *flammable goods*. If items such as paint, adhesives, oil or chemicals are stored or used on your premises they should be kept in a separate store room and well away from any source of heat. Aerosols, gas cartridges and cylinders, if exposed to heat, can explode and start fires
- *heaters*. Portable heaters, such as the sort used in restaurants and offices to supplement the general heating, can be the cause of a fire if goods come into close contact with them or if they are accidentally knocked over. Never place books, papers or clothes over convector or storage heaters, as this can cause them to overheat and can result in a fire.

Preventing fires

Being alert to the potential hazard of fire can help prevent emergencies. Potential fire hazards exist in every area of the workplace, so regular preventative checks are essential as part of your everyday working practice.

- As far as possible, switch off and unplug all electrical equipment when it is not being used. Some equipment may be designed to be permanently connected to the mains (eg. video recorders with digital clocks); always check the manufacturer's instructions.
- If new equipment is being installed, ensure this is carried out properly and arrange a system of regular maintenance.
- Electrical equipment is covered by British Safety Standards, so look for plugs that conform to BS1 363 and fuses that conform to BS1362.
- Ensure there are sufficient ash trays available for smokers to use.

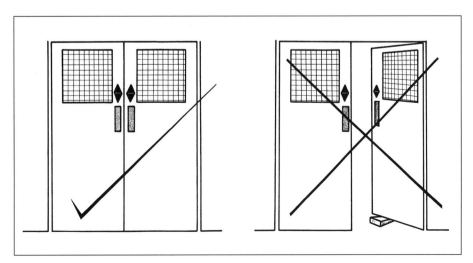

Fire doors used correctly (left) and incorrectly (right)

- Inspect all public rooms, kitchens, staff rooms and store rooms to ensure all discarded smoking equipment is collected in lidded metal bins and not mixed with other waste.
- As often as possible, look behind cushions and down the side of seats to check a cigarette end has not been dropped by mistake.
- Ensure rooms and corridors are free of waste and rubbish, especially in areas where litter tends to collect, such as in corners and underneath stairwells.
- Place all accumulated waste in appropriate receptacles, away from the main building.
- Check that all external stairways and means of escape are kept clear.
- Make sure that fire doors and smoke stop doors on escape routes are regularly maintained. These doors are designed to withstand heat and to reduce the risks from smoke. They must not be wedged open or prevented from working properly in the event of a fire.

IN THE KITCHEN AND RESTAURANT

Fire hazards

In a kitchen or restaurant there are additional hazards that you should be aware of. These areas, the kitchen in particular, tend to get hot and fires can easily start. Note the following points:

- Frying operations should be kept under constant supervision.
- Electrical cooking equipment (eg. deep fat fryers) with faulty controls or thermostats can cause any oil or fat being used to overheat, ignite and cause a fire. All equipment must be maintained and kept free from build-up of grease or dirt. Check that extraction hoods and grease traps are cleaned and maintained regularly (see Unit 1ND1, pages 47–55).
- Cloths, aprons and loose clothing should be kept away from any open flames on a stove. It is very easy for fabric to catch alight and cause a fire to spread.
- Gas cylinders, used perhaps in the restaurant, should be in good condition and undamaged. Staff using the cylinders must be thoroughly trained in their use and aware of dangers from inadequate storage and damage to the cylinders.
- Any CO_2 cylinders must be properly secured and free from damage.
- If candles are used in the restaurant, care must be taken to ensure they are kept away from flammable material.
- If there is an open fire in the restaurant, customers, visitors and staff must be protected from the flames by a fire guard.

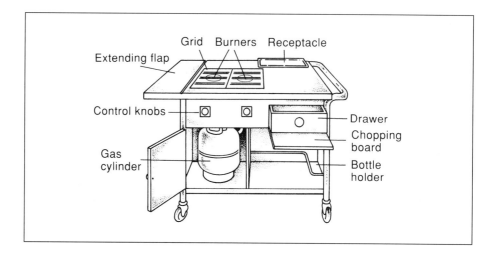

Gueridon trolley showing gas cylinder in place

Fire safety conditions

The following conditions must always be met within a working area.
- Fire doors should not be hooked or wedged open (see p. 9). Check that they close automatically when released. Fire stop doors held by magnets need to be closed from 11 pm–7 am.
- Fire extinguishers should be available, full and not damaged.
- Fire exit doors should be easy to use and secure.
- Emergency lighting should be maintained and visible at all times. Make sure that the lights are not obscured by screens, drapes, clothing, etc.
- Signs and fire notices giving details of exit routes must be available in all areas and kept in good condition.
- Alarms should be readily accessible and free from obstruction.
- Fire sprinklers and smoke detectors must be kept clear of obstruction for at least 60 cm (24 in) in all directions.
- Fire exit doors and routes must be kept clear at all times and in a good state of repair.

Do this

- Carry out a full survey of your own work area and identify any potential fire hazards. List the hazards under the following categories: combustible material, flammable liquids, flammable gases, electrical hazards.
- Discuss the potential dangers with your colleagues and agree ways of minimising the risk.
- Revise your own working methods to minimise fire risks.

Discovering a fire

If you discover a fire, follow the sequence of events given below:
1 sound the alarm immediately
2 call the fire brigade
3 evacuate the area
4 assemble in the designated safe area for roll call.

Sounding the alarm

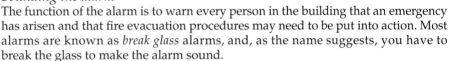
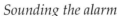

The function of the alarm is to warn every person in the building that an emergency has arisen and that fire evacuation procedures may need to be put into action. Most alarms are known as *break glass* alarms, and, as the name suggests, you have to break the glass to make the alarm sound.

Calling the fire brigade

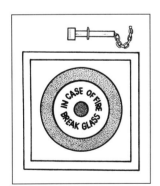

A break glass alarm

The responsibility for calling the fire brigade falls to different people in different establishments. Often it is a receptionist or telephonist who will be expected to deal with the call. Make sure that you know who is responsible for this in your establishment.

When calling the fire brigade, be ready with the following information:
- your establishment's address
- your establishment's telephone number
- the precise location of the fire.

You may like to write down the necessary information about the establishment and keep it near the telephone in case of an emergency. If you do have to make an emergency phone call, make sure that you listen for the address to be repeated back to you before replacing the telephone receiver.

Evacuating the area and assembling outside

It is essential for everyone to be able to escape from danger. If you do not have specific duties to carry out in the evacuation procedures you should leave the premises immediately on hearing the alarm.

When evacuating the premises:
- switch off equipment and machinery
- close windows and doors behind you
- follow marked escape routes
- remain calm, do not run
- assist others in their escape
- go immediately to an allocated assembly point
- do not return for belongings, no matter how valuable.

You and all of your colleagues should be instructed on what to do if fire breaks out. Customers and visitors should also be made aware of what to do in the event of a fire and made familiar with the means of escape provided. This is usually done by means of notices in all public areas and rooms. Where foreign staff work, notices should be printed in the most appropriate languages.

Fighting fires

Fighting fires can be a dangerous activity, and is generally to be discouraged. Personal safety and safe evacuation must always be your primary concern. If a fire does break out, it should only be tackled in its very early stages and before it has started to spread.

Before you tackle a fire:
- evacuate everyone and follow the emergency procedure to alert the fire brigade. Tell someone that you are attempting to tackle the fire
- always put your own and other people's safety first; never risk injury to fight fires. Always make sure you can escape if you need to and remember that smoke can kill. Remember the rule: *if in doubt, get out*
- never let a fire get between you and the way out. If you have any doubt about whether the extinguisher is suitable for the fire do not use it; leave immediately
- remember that fire extinguishers are only for 'first aid' fire fighting. Never attempt to tackle the fire if it is beginning to spread or if the room is filling with smoke
- if you cannot put out the fire, or your extinguisher runs out, leave immediately, closing doors and windows as you go.

Fire fighting equipment

Types

On-premise fire fighting equipment is designed to be used for small fires only and is very specific to the type of fire. Hand extinguishers are designed to be easy to use, but can require practice and training in how to use them.

All fire fighting equipment is designed to remove one of the three factors needed for a fire: heat, oxygen or flammable material. Fire extinguishers are filled with one of the following:
- *water*. This type of extinguisher provides a powerful and efficient means of putting out fires involving wood, paper and fabric
- *dry powder*. These extinguishers can be used to put out wood, paper, fabric and flammable liquid fires, but are more generally used for fires involving electrical equipment
- *foam*. The pre-mix foam extinguishers use a combination of water and aqueous film, and are effective for extinguishing paper, wood, fabric and flammable liquid fires

---

MEMORY JOGGER

What are the different types of on-site fire fighting equipment and the type of fires they can help control?

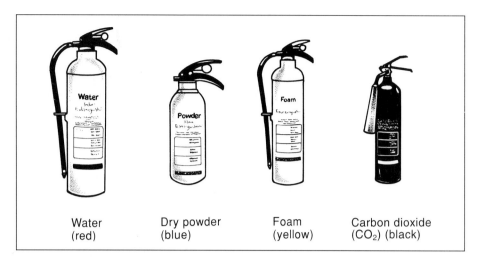

Water (red)   Dry powder (blue)   Foam (yellow)   Carbon dioxide (CO₂) (black)

Fire extinguishers

- *carbon dioxide*. These extinguishers are not commonly in use, but can be used in situations where there are flammable oils and spirits, and in offices where there is electronic equipment.

Fire regulations

1 Fire extinguishers must be wall mounted on wall brackets (unless designed specifically to be floor standing) and should not be used as door stops.
2 When a fire extinguisher is discharged it must be replenished as soon as possible, and at least within 24 hours.
3 Every establishment should have a scale drawing indicating the location of fire fighting equipment.

Fire blankets are also used to extinguish fires. These are made from a variety of materials: some are made of woven fibreglass while others have a fibreglass base and are coated with silicone rubber on both sides. Fire blankets are generally housed in a wall mounted plastic pack with a quick-pull front opening.

How to use a fire blanket

An establishment may also have fire hoses which are linked to the water supply. These can be used in the same situations as the red water based extinguishers and are usually activated by the action of removing the hose from it's mounting.

Case study

You are carrying out a security check of your establishment and you notice that two of the fire extinguishers have been removed from their wall brackets and the fire exit near the delivery area is blocked with old cardboard boxes.

1   What would be your main concern if you found these problems?

2   What would be the immediate action you would take?

3   What would be the longer term action that could be taken to prevent this happening again?

Maintaining equipment

Fire fighting equipment is essential in areas where there is a potential risk from fires. It is essential that equipment is:

● *maintained regularly and kept in good condition.* The fire brigade or your supplier will carry out annual checks and note on the extinguisher when the check was carried out

● *kept clear from obstruction at all times.* The equipment must be visible and readily available. Obstructions can prevent easy access and may result in unnecessary damage to the equipment

● *available in all areas of work.* Different types of extinguishers are needed for different fires, so the most suitable extinguisher should be available in the area. Guidance can be sought from the fire brigade or equipment suppliers

● *used by trained operators.* Fire extinguishers can be quite noisy and powerful and can startle you if you have not used one before. It is important that the user knows the best way of utilising the extinguisher to tackle a fire in the most effective way.

Finding out about fire legislation

The fire legislation has been developed to ensure premises and working practices are safe for employees, customers and visitors. As mentioned in the introduction, failure to observe the regulations can lead to damage to property and, in more serious situations, loss of life. The legislation has been developed for everyone's safety and everyone has a role in ensuring they do not ignore fire notices, information provided about fire exits ;and ensure they take part in fire evacuations and fire drills when necessary.

In your work area there will be notices and information posted around the building. Details about the fire regulations will also be kept on site for you, your manager of your supervisor to refer to.

The local Fire Station will have a nominated Fire Officer who gives advice and guidance to establishments on how well they are complying with the regulations and identify any improvements in the evacuation drill that may be needed. The local Fire Officer will also be keen to give advice and support and, where appropriate, assist in the training of staff within the business.

Do this

● Find out where your nearest fire exits are located and the route you need to follow to reach your nominated assembly point.

● Identify the fire extinguishers available in your area and learn how to use them.

● Look out for potential fire hazards in your area and remove or report them immediately.

● Take part in practice fire drills in your establishment and learn to recognise the type of sound made by the alarm in your building.

What have you learned

1 What are the possible causes of fire in the working environment?
2 What is the first thing you should do on discovering a fire?
3 What type of extinguisher would you use for putting out:
   ● An electrical fire?
   ● A fire in a deep fat fryer?
   ● A fire in a store room where chemicals are stored?
4 List four points you need to remember when evacuating your department if the fire alarm sounds.
5 Why is it important to comply with your establishments' fire regulations?
6 How does a fire blanket work in preventing a fire from spreading?
7 Why should fire escapes and exits be kept free from rubbish and doors unlocked when people are on the premises?

ELEMENT 3: Maintain a safe environment for customers, staff and visitors

INTRODUCTION

The safety of everyone who works or visits an establishment should he foremost in the minds of everyone. As a main part of any employee's work they have to carry out procedures and comply with regulations which have been designed to ensure good working practices and to reduce the risk of injury to themselves and others. These regulations are also designed to make the working environment more comfortable and safe to work in.

The Health and Safety at Work Act (1974) set out to detail the responsibilities of employees and employers to take a 'general duty of care' and to place an emphasis on the need for preventative measures to he enacted and managed. The act encouraged the constant re-evaluation of systems and processes which prevent accidents and reduce risks to everyone in the establishment.

The Health and Safety at Work Act (1974) is an 'enabling' Act in that it imposes a general duty of care, but has the flexibility to be adapted to suit future needs. Regulations passed under the 1974 Act include, so far:
● Health and Safety (First Aid) Regulations (1981)
● Reporting of injuries, diseases and dangerous occurrences 1985 (RIDDOR)
● Control of substances hazardous to health regulations 1988 (COSHH)

Under the *Health and Safety at Work Act* (HASAWA 1974) there are certain responsibilities both employers and employees must comply with. Those given below are ones you should be particularly aware of.

Employers' responsibilities
Employers must, as far as is reasonably practicable:
● provide and maintain plants and systems of work that are safe and without risks to health
● make arrangements to ensure safety and the absence of risks to health in connection with the use, handling, storage and transport of articles and substances
● provide such information, instruction, training and supervision as will ensure the health and safety of employees
● maintain any place of work under their control in a safe condition without risks to health and provide at least statutory welfare facilities and arrangements.

These duties also extend to include customers and others visiting the premises.

MEMORY JOGGER

What are the employees' responsibilities under the Health and Safety Act 1974?

15

Employees' responsibilities

As an employee you also have responsibilities and must:

● take reasonable care of your own health and safety
● take reasonable care for the health and safety of other people who may be affected by what you do or neglect to do at work
● cooperate with the establishment in the steps it takes to meet its legal duties
● report any physical conditions or systems which you consider unsafe or potentially unsafe to a supervisor.

These responsibilities have been drawn up for the benefit of everyone in the workplace, to ensure that the risk of accident or injury to anyone is minimised through promotion of a thoughtful and considerate approach to work practices.

Many working days can be lost through accidents, which more often than not are caused through carelessness and thoughtlessness. As a result, the business suffers reduced productivity and, in serious cases, considerable trading time if forced to close while the premises are made safe.

Under the HASAWA, Health and Safety inspectors (often under the umbrella of the Environmental Health Office) have the authority to place prohibition notices on premises if they persistently fail to meet the standards set by law. This might occur if there were a physical problem in the building or in equipment, or an outbreak of food poisoning caused by poor hygiene practice.

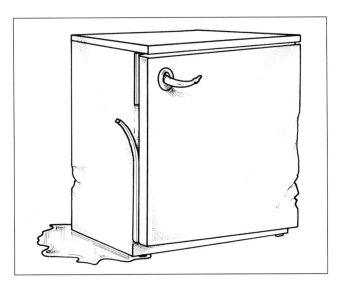

A damaged refrigerator

Whatever the cause, it is important that you and your colleagues have a positive and active approach to maintaining the safety of the environment in which you operate.

The Health and Safety Executive has the responsibility of advising on safety matters and of enforcing the HASAWA if the obligations of this Act are not met. This is one reason why serious accidents must always be reported to the Executive.

In the case of hotel and catering establishments, Local Authorities appoint their own inspectors: Environmental Health Officers (EHOs) who work with companies and colleges on matters associated with health and safety.

Health and Safety Inspectors

These appointed representatives have a number of powers under the Act which include:

● being able to enter premises at reasonable times

- to test, measure, photograph and examine as they see fit
- to take samples or dismantle equipment
- to view H&S records, accident books etc
- to serve *Improvement Notices* requiring action within a period of not less than 21 days
- to prosecute *any* person contravening a statutory provision (penalty is a maximum fine of £5,000 and/or term of imprisonment up to 2 years).

HAZARDS

Cautionary measures

Sign warning of potential hazard

1 When you spot a hazard, if practicable, remove it immediately and report the situation to your supervisor. Most organisations have a standard Health and Safety Report Form stating action to be taken and follow up procedures.
   If you are unable to remove the hazard, as in the case of a doorway blocked by a delivery of goods, monitor the situation and if it appears the goods are not to be moved quickly, report the problem to your supervisor.

   By taking immediate action over a potential hazard you will be contributing to your own wellbeing and that of your colleagues. Some hazards, however, may be due to poor working practices or faulty building design and they will need a different approach and more time to solve.
2 You may also need to place signs, such as 'Caution Wet Floor' to warn others of the potential hazard they are approaching. In some cases you may even need to cordon off an area whilst you deal with, or make arrangements to deal with the hazard.
3 Other cautionary measures will include ensuring you keep potentially dangerous items such as chemicals under lock and key, or out of reach of others.
4 Take note of all signs warning of dangers or potential hazards, especially those associated with:
   - use of machinery
   - hazardous chemicals
   - cleaning fluids.

In some instances you may need to draw the attention of others to the signs.

Essential knowledge	Preventative action should always be taken quickly when a hazard is spotted, in order to ● prevent injury to staff and customers ● prevent damage to buildings and staff ● comply with the law.

Hazard spotting

Much of the health and safety legislation is aimed at preventing accidents from happening and ensuring the environment is safe for everyone within it.

A *hazard* is defined as something with potential to cause harm. A *risk* can be expressed as the likelihood of that harm actually arising.

Some of the most common causes of accidents in the workplace are caused through basic mistakes, such as someone not cleaning up a spillage, or a cable left trailing across a walkway.

By being aware of the potential danger of hazards you will be able to contribute effectively to the safety of the area in which you work. The 'safety points' guidelines that follow show areas in which you can start contributing towards maintaining a safe environment.

Safety points to remember
- Be constantly aware of obstacles on the floor or in corridors and remove them, returning them to their rightful place.
- Watch out for damaged floor coverings: it is very easy to catch your heel and trip over.
- Make sure electrical cables or wires never run across walkways. Always keep them behind you when you are working to reduce the risk of damage to them.
- Clean up spillages as soon as they occur. If grease is spilt use salt or sand to absorb the spillage before cleaning the area.
- If cleaning up spillages use wet floor signs to warn people of the danger.
- Never handle electrical plugs with wet hands. *Water conducts electricity: this can cause death.*
- Never use equipment that appears faulty or damaged. You are increasing the risk to yourself by doing so. Report the problem immediately and ensure the equipment is repaired.
- Use a stepladder to reach to the top of shelves. Never stand on piles of cases or boxes.
- If lifting a load, make sure it is not too heavy or awkward for you to move on your own. If you need help, ask. Back injuries are one of the most common reasons for people having to take time out from work.

Case study

The area in which you are working is very busy throughout the day and there are occasionally items of food dropped on the floor. One day, just before the main lunch service is due to go out one of the team drops some soup on to the floor. He mops up the spillage quickly but is aware it needs to be more fully cleaned to reduce the risks to his colleagues.

1 What are the main risks this spillage presents to the team in the kitchen?
2 What cautionary measures would you expect your colleague to carry out in this situation?
3 What steps should you take to ensure you are complying with your responsibilities under the HASAW Act?

Kitchen hazards

In the kitchen area there are some special hazards to be aware of. The following points show how these can be kept to a minimum.
- Always use the correct knife for the job you are doing. Use of incorrect knives can lead to accidents. Always leave a knife with its blade flat: if you leave the blade uppermost it would be very easy for you or a colleague to put a hand down on top of the blade and cut the palm of the hand. Never leave a knife immersed in water.
- If walking while carrying knives, always point the blade towards the floor, away from your body. If you were to trip or fall you might end up stabbing someone or injuring yourself. (See also Unit 1ND2: *Handle and Maintain Knives*, pages 56–64.)
- Remember that slicing machines should always be used by trained operators and with the safety guard in place. The machinery must be cleaned by someone over the age of 18. (See also Unit 2ND17: *Clean cutting equipment*, pages 90–94).
- Always use a dry cloth when handling hot containers as wet cloths can transmit heat and burn you, causing you to drop boiling liquid on yourself.
- Think carefully about how you position pans on the stove. Keep handles away from the heat and do not let them protrude over the edge of the stove where they can easily be knocked off.

Much of the health and safety legislation focuses on people having a thoughtful and commonsense approach to their work and the safety of others. Many of the accidents which happen on premises, whether it be to staff, customers or visitors, occur as a direct result of someone not doing the right thing at the right time.

Hazardous substances

The *Control of Substances Hazardous to Health Regulations (1988)* (COSHH) form part of the Health and Safety Regulations and lay down the essential requirements and a step-by-step approach to protecting people exposed to them. In the kitchen, the most likely exposure to chemicals is through the use of cleaning and associated chemicals.

The COSHH regulations set out the measures employers and employees have to take. Failure to comply with COSHH constitutes an offence and is subject to penalties under the *Health and Safety at Work Act 1974.*

Substances hazardous to health include:
1   those labelled as dangerous (eg. toxic, corrosive)
2   those where exposure over a long time is thought dangerous (eg. pesticides)
3   harmful micro-organisms
4   substantial concentration of dust of any kind
5   any material, mixture or compound used at work, or arising from work activities, which can harm people's health.

In the kitchen, hazardous substances may include eg. bleach, ammonia, chlorine, detergents, methylated spirits, solvents, cleaning fluid.

COSHH requires an employer to:
● assess the risk to health arising and state the precautions needed
● introduce appropriate measures to prevent or control the risk
● ensure the control measures are used
● where necessary, monitor the exposure of employees
● to inform and instruct employees on a regular basis.

COSHH requires an employee to:
● know what risks there are in using certain substances
● understand how these risks are controlled
● take the necessary precautions.

When storing hazardous substances it is important:
● they are stored in a locked area
● they are clearly labelled in a securely capped container
● to have First Aid instructions and method of summoning assistance
● to have a system of work related to their use.

Reporting hazards

Under the HASAW Act, every company must have a procedure in place for employees to report potential hazards they have identified. In some companies there may be *Safety Representatives* whose role is to bring the hazard to the supervisor's attention. The Safety Representative may be part of a *Health and Safety Committee* who will meet regularly to deal with matters of safety and to ensure appropriate action is taken.

Your department may have a standard *Hazard Report Form* which you would complete to help you and your supervisor deal with the hazard through a formalised procedure. You may also be involved in carrying out regular safety audits in your department aimed at ensuring that planned preventative work is implemented.

Under *The Health and Safety at Work Act* it is your responsibility to be aware of potential hazards and to take the necessary action to prevent them from becoming actual hazards.

Do this

- Carry out a hazard spotting tour of your area highlighting potential dangers and noting any actions needed.
- Find out how you are required to report health and safety hazards in your place of work.
- Examine the equipment you use in your department. Is the wiring in good condition? When was the equipment last serviced? Discuss any problems found with your supervisor.

DEALING WITH SUSPICIOUS ITEMS AND PACKAGES

In any area of work there may be times when an unattended item, package or bag raises suspicion. This could lead to an emergency, and, if not handled correctly, may result in danger or injury to people in the area.

It is important to treat any suspicious item seriously. Be aware of the dangers it potentially contains and be prepared to inform people of your suspicions quickly and calmly.

A suspicious package which is not dealt with immediately may result in serious injury to people in the area or serious damage to the building. It is an essential part of your daily work to keep alert to dangers from suspect packages and follow laid down procedures when dealing with the problem.

<table>
<tr><td>

MEMORY JOGGER

What are the actions to take if you discover a suspicious item in or around your area of work?

</td></tr>
</table>

Recognising a suspicious item or package

It is difficult to give precise guidance about where you may discover a suspicious package, or what size or shape it might be. Either of the types of package described below might raise your suspicions: in fact, anything that sticks out in your mind as somewhat unusual.
- Something that has been left unattended for some time.
- Something that looks out of place, like a man's holdall in the ladies' cloakroom, or a full carrier bag near a rubbish bin.

On discovering a suspicious item

- Do not attempt to move or touch the item. The action of moving or disturbing the item may be enough to start off a reaction leading to an explosion or fire.

A full carrier bag left next to an empty rubbish bin might be enough to arouse suspicions

- Remain calm and composed. Try not to cause panic by shouting an alarm or running from the item. People and property can be injured through a disorderly or panicked evacuation.
- Report the matter to your supervisor or the police immediately. Check your establishment's procedures to find out who you should inform.
- If possible, cordon off the area and move people away. It may be difficult to do this without causing people in the area to panic, but it is essential that no one attempts to move or touch the item, so you will need to warn people to keep clear.
- At some point it may be necessary to evacuate the building, or the part of the building nearest to the suspect package. This may be a decision taken by your supervisor, or the police if they are involved. If it is thought necessary to clear the area, follow your company procedures for the evacuation of the building.

Essential knowledge

- Suspicious items or packages must never be approached or tampered with in case they contain explosive materials which may be set off.
- Suspicious items or packages must always be reported immediately to prevent serious accidents occurring involving bombs and explosives.

Reporting a suspicious item

If you are reporting a suspicious item make sure you are able to tell your contact:

1 what the suspicious package looks like:

'It's a small brown suitcase about two foot square with a black strap around it – it looks locked.'

2 the exact location of the suspect device:

'The suitcase is in the main goods received area, on the right as you enter.'

3 the precautions you have taken so far:

'I've told the kitchen team and asked the cleaner to put wet floor signs near it to keep people away'

4 the existence of any known hazards in the surrounding area, eg. gas points:

'As far as I know the area around the package is clear from any supply lines.'

5 the reason for your suspicion:

6 any witnesses to the placing of the package or item:

Do this

- Carry out a survey of your work area to identify places where suspicious items or packages could be left.
- Find out what procedures your establishment follows for dealing with suspect packages.
- Carry out regular checks in your area.

DEALING WITH AN ACCIDENT

Within the normal course of your work you may be required to deal with an accident or an emergency resulting in someone sustaining an injury. Often these injuries are not life-threatening, but occasionally they may be serious enough to warrant the person involved being taken to hospital, or being unable to carry on their work for that day.

Most organisations have several people trained in dealing with emergencies and administering first aid. These *first aiders* are often spread around the different departments to ensure that someone is available at all times. Organisations are legally required to have trained first aiders on the premises and to display a list detailing their place of work and contact telephone number on notice boards.

First aiders are usually the people who deal with an emergency before a doctor or an ambulance arrives (if necessary). They have a responsibility to respond to emergencies as they arise, and are trained to diagnose the course of action needed to deal with the injured person. You should immediately call a first aider when an accident occurs.

Recording an accident

All accidents need to be reported as soon after the event as is practicable. Any accident is required by law to be reported and recorded in an accident book located on the premises. Any accident resulting in serious injury must be reported to the Health and Safety Executive within three working days. Your establishment should have procedures for dealing with this.

In the case of an accident to a member of staff, ideally the person who received the injury would complete the accident book. However, it may be necessary for an appointed person to report the accident on their behalf.

The following information is mandatory:
1 the date and time of the accident
2 the particulars of the person affected:
   ● full name
   ● occupation
   ● nature of injury or condition
3 where the accident happened
4 a brief description of the circumstances.

If an accident happens to a customer or visitor there will probably be different records available. Check on the type of records kept by your own establishment.

Accident record keeping is important, not only to comply with the legal requirements under health and safety legislation, but also to ensure details are available for possible insurance claims. Accident reporting can also be a great help when analysing trends and identifying where there may be a need for preventative training.

Complying with the regulations related to accidents

The current regulations governing the notification and recording of accidents are contained in the *Reporting of Injuries, Diseases and Dangerous Occurrences Regulations 1985 (RIDDOR)*. These regulations are about ensuring that a company has procedures in place to manage the reporting of accidents. They are separated into five main areas:
1 Fatal or specified major accidents or conditions
2 Notifiable 'over three days' injuries
3 Reportable diseases
4 Dangerous occurrences (whether there is an injury or not)
5 Other accidents.

Each establishment is responsible for ensuring there are procedures in place which enable employees to comply with the regulations. Failure to follow the RIDDOR requirements can lead to prosecution under the Act.

Do this

● Establish where the Accident Recording Book is located.
● Find out whether there are different procedures and records for accidents involving customers and visitors to those involving staff for your establishment.
● Find out the procedure for reporting accidents to the emergency services.

Who is a first aider

The term *first aider* describes any person who has received a certificate from an authorised training body indicating that they are qualified to render First Aid. The term was first used in 1894 by the voluntary First Aid organisations and certificates are now offered by St John Ambulance, St Andrew's Ambulance Association and the British Red Cross. The certificate is only valid for three years, to ensure that first aiders are highly trained, regularly examined and kept up to date in their knowledge and skills.

First Aid organisations (left to right): St John Ambulance, St Andrew's Ambulance Association, British Red Cross

Once the first aider is dealing with the casualty their main aims are to:
● preserve life
● prevent the condition worsening
● promote recovery.

Their responsibility is to:
● assess the situation
● carry out diagnosis of the casualty
● give immediate, appropriate and adequate treatment
● arrange, without delay, for the casualty to be taken to a hospital or to see a doctor if appropriate.

Giving information to the first aider

Once the first aider arrives at the accident they will need certain information from you before they begin their treatment.

Be prepared to tell them as much as you know about:
● *the history of the accident*. How the accident happened, whether the person has been moved, what caused the injury
● *the symptoms*. Where the casualty is feeling pain, what other signs you have observed, whether the symptoms have changed
● *the treatment given*. What has already been done to the casualty and whether to the best of your knowledge, the casualty has any other illness or is receiving treatment or medication.

Initial response to an accident

MEMORY JOGGER

What would you do if you were not a first aider and you were in the vicinity when someone had an accident?

Whether you are a first aider or not, in the event of an accident it is the initial response to the situation and the way laid-down procedures are followed that can make the difference to the treatment received by the injured person.

You need to know what immediate response you should give if a person near you sustains an injury. Many of the points are common sense, and will depend upon the extent of the accident and the speed with which you can contact the relevant people.

When dealing with accidents the following points are important.
● *Remain calm when approaching the injured person*. The injured person will probably be frightened by the situation they are in, or may be in pain, and they will benefit from someone taking control of the situation. This may help reduce the feeling of panic, helplessness or embarrassment they may be experiencing.
● *Offer reassurance and comfort*. Keep the casualty (if conscious) informed of the actions you are taking by talking in a quiet, confident manner. Do not move the person but keep them warm, covering them with a blanket, or a coat if necessary. By keeping them warm you are minimising the risk of shock which can often cause the condition of the injured person to deteriorate. By preventing them from moving you are allowing time for them to recover and reducing the possibility of further injury.
● *Do not give them anything to drink*. If the casualty is given something to drink they may not be able to have an anaesthetic if necessary. A drink may also make them feel worse and may cause nausea.
● *Contact or instruct someone else to contact a first aider.*
● *Stay by the casualty* if you can, to reassure them and ensure they do not cause further injury to themselves.
● *Minimise the risk of danger* to yourself, the injured and other people in the area.

In the case of:
● *gas or poisonous fumes*: if possible, cut off the source.
● *electrical contact*: break the contact either by removing the injured person from the source, or removing the source. Do this by using something that does not conduct electricity, such as a wooden broom handle. Make sure that you do not come into contact with the electrical source yourself. Take precautions against further contact.

- *fire, or collapsing buildings*: move the casualty to a safe area after temporarily immobilising the injured part of the person.

Do this

- Find out the name and work location of your nearest first aider (a list should be displayed in your work area).
- Find out how you can acquire training in First Aid.

Contacting the emergency services

If you or your supervisor decide that assistance is required from the emergency services, or you have been asked to call them by the first aider, you will need to pass on certain information:

1 *your telephone number*, so that if for any reason you are cut off, the officer will then be able to contact you
2 *the exact location of the incident*. This will help the ambulance or doctor to get to the scene of the accident more quickly
3 *an indication of the type and seriousness of the accident*. This will allow the team to bring the most appropriate equipment and call for back-up if necessary
4 *the number, sex and approximate age of the casualties involved*. If possible, you should also explain the nature of their injuries
5 *any special help you feel is needed*. For example, in cases where you suspect a heart attack.

It might be a good idea to write down the information you need to pass on before calling the emergency services.

If you do call 999, you will be asked to state the service required: in the case of accidents you would normally state 'ambulance'. The officer responding to your call will be able to pass on messages to any other emergency services necessary, such as gas or fire.

Establishment procedures
Procedures vary from company to company as to who has authority to call the emergency services so it is important that you find out how you are expected to deal with the situation in your own place of work.

Correct lifting techniques

One of the most common sickness problems related to work is back injury. It affects not only those in manual jobs, but also it can affect sedentary workers. Under the Health and Safety Regulations, the *Manual Handling Operations Regulations* are intended to reduce the risk of injury and sets out simple steps to take to reduce such injury. Back injury can put people out of work for a while as well as having a long term debilitating effect on a person's health. Prevention of back injury is a *must*.

When lifting at work where there is a risk of injury, there are a number of questions to consider. For example, in the longer term:
- can the lifting operation be eliminated?
- is the lifting operation unnecessary?
- could the lifting operation be automated?
- could the lifting operation be mechanised?

As well as these longer term issues it is also important an employee gives thought to how they are going to move an object – before they do it. They could:
- 'walk the route' to check how to lift and move the object without causing injury
- get someone else to help if the load is heavy

- get someone else to help if the load is bulky or an awkward shape
- use lifting techniques which do not put strain on the back (eg. see illustration).

If an employee is required to lift as part of their job under Health and Safety legislation it is important they are trained in manual handling techniques, and, having been trained, it is then the responsibility of the employee to work to the laid down procedures. The pictures below illustrate the correct way of lifting heavy objects.

The correct way to lift a heavy object

DISCLOSABLE INFORMATION

During the time you are at work there may be people who ask you questions. These may be general questions about the operation of the bar or restaurant, or may be specific about one aspect of the business. It is important when this happens you are discreet and careful about what you say. It may be by answering these questions there could be a breach of security, or have a more indirect effect on the business (eg. an idea being used by a competitor).

If you are unsure what you can or can't say to someone about the business or how it operates, it is best to say nothing and to check with your manager or supervisor. It is also a useful idea to mention to your manager or supervisor about the questions you have been asked. It may alert him or her and avoid a problem in the future.

REPORTING UNUSUAL / NON-ROUTINE INCIDENTS

Throughout the working day it is likely you and your colleagues have been busy. Much of the work we do does involve patterns of work and routines. If something disturbs that routine or seems out of the ordinary it is important these incidents are reported to the appropriate person (usually your manager or supervisor).

It may be that the incident does need further action to be taken, but it also may result in a bigger problem being avoided. In cases where you see something which is a little bit out of the ordinary it is important it is reported.

FINDING OUT ABOUT AND COMPLYING WITH THE REGULATIONS

Health and Safety is the responsibility of us all. Failure to comply with the requirements laid down in the Acts may lead to an occurrence which could lead to prosecution. An injured person may be able to sue their employer, or a fellow employee, for breach of their statutory duty. This could lead to damages being awarded through the Civil Courts, or to them being prosecuted in the Criminal Court.

Information about the Health and Safety aspects of your work should be made available by your manager or supervisor. There may be a *Health and Safety at Work Handbook* available when you join an establishment, detailing your responsibilities and those of your colleagues. There will also be information available in the form of posters, statutory notices posted around the building, and on staff notice boards. You should read these and make a point of checking if any of them have been updated.

During training sessions you will be given information about the regulations and how they affect your work. You should also be given guidance on working practices (such as lifting techniques) which will ensure you do not put yourself or others at risk from injury.

Case study

You have just finished your training and have started work in a hotel. You are in the kitchen with one other colleague when he accidentally knocks a large pan of boiling liquid. It slops over, scalding his hands badly, which puts out the gas.
1 *What should you do first?*
2 *Who should you go to for help?*
3 *Who is responsible for calling an ambulance? What information should you give the emergency services?*
4 *Who should fill out the Accident Register?*

What have you learned

1 Why is it important you are aware of your responsibilities under the *Health and Safety at Work (1974) Act*?
2 What are the main responsibilities for employees under the HASAWA?
3 Why is it important to be involved and carry out hazard spotting exercises?
4 Why is it important to report any suspicious packages or items you may spot?
5 What might make you become suspicious about a package or item?
6 Why must accidents by reported?
7 Where can you find the Accident Register (Book) in your establishment?
8 Why is it important to use correct lifting techniques?
9 Who can provide you with up to date information about health and safety matters?
10 List five potential health and safety hazards in your area of work.

ELEMENT 4: Maintain a secure environment for customers, staff and visitors

INTRODUCTION

UXBRIDGE COLLEGE LIBRARY

Maintaining effective security should be the concern of everyone working within an establishment and is an essential part of good business practice. There may be staff within your own organisation employed as *Security Officers* whose role will include all aspects of protecting people on the premises, looking after the security of the building and the property contained within it.

Effective security practices can help protect the profit of the business by reducing the likelihood of losses through, for example:
● *theft*, whether through break-ins causing damage to the building or through walk-outs where customers leave without paying for their service
● *fraud*, by customers or staff
● *missing stock*.

Profitability can be affected both by the immediate loss of property or damage to the building and by bad publicity, which can damage the business through loss of custom.

Your role

Whether or not there are security staff employed within your organisation, you will find there are many situations within your working day where you need to be security conscious. It is easy to become complacent or lazy in your working habits, which can lead to an opportunity being seen and seized by a thief. A common example of this is a member of staff leaving a storage area unlocked and people being able to gain access easily.

Daily work patterns may also present an opportunity to be exploited by a thief. When we work in an area we become familiar with our surroundings, used to seeing things in a certain place and following procedures in a certain way. It is often these patterns that are observed by potential thieves and which can lead to break-ins or thefts.

Being aware of potential breaches of security and knowing how to report them or the action to take is an essential starting point. Think about the way you work and how security conscious you are. Make sure that you always follow the basic security practices listed below.
● Keep display materials beyond the reach of any customers and as far away from main entrances as possible, making it difficult for people to remove the items without being spotted.
● Keep security issues and procedures confidential: you can never be sure who might overhear you discussing a sensitive issue.
● Keep your own belongings, such as handbags or wallets, secure and out of sight in a locked compartment or drawer.
● Keep alert to anything or anyone which looks suspicious, for example: an occupied car parked outside the building for a long period of time, boxes or ladders placed near to windows, fire exits left open.
● Keep keys, especially master keys, under close supervision. You will probably find that your establishment has a log book for recording the issue of keys.

It is important for you to follow any particular security procedures that are in place in your establishment. These procedures are often there both for your benefit and to minimise any loss to the business.

Do this

● Think about your working day. List the things you do where attention to security is essential.
● Now write down your ideas for improving security within your job. Discuss your ideas with your supervisor.
● Find out what security procedures you are required to follow within your work area.

Keys, property and areas should be secured from unauthorised access at all times in order to:
- prevent theft
- prevent damage to property
- prevent damage to the business from customer loss of confidence.

Dealing with lost or missing property

From time to time company, customer or staff property may go missing. This can be due to a variety of reasons, such as:
- customer property may have been left behind in a guest room or public area
- company property may have been moved without people knowing and may, in fact, be misplaced rather than lost
- a member of staff may have been careless about returning property, such as dirty linen to the linen room, or crockery to the crockery store
- items may have been stolen from the property. You may hear this type of loss called *shrinkage* or *pilfering*, especially when referring to food or liquor missing from refrigerators or cellars.

In most establishments there will be procedures for dealing with any missing property. If you discover that property has gone missing it is important you follow the correct procedure. The type of information you should report will probably include:
- a description of the missing item/s
- the date and time you discovered the item/s were missing
- the location where item/s are normally stored
- details of any searches or actions taken to locate the item/s.

In some cases your organisation may decide to report the loss to the police. This is common where the item missing is of value or where a substantial amount of goods has gone missing. In some organisations all losses are reported to the police whether theft is thought probable or not. If the police are involved, you may be required to give them information, so it is essential for you to be clear on the circumstances of the losses.

Case study

A customer has been to you to report that she thinks someone has stolen her handbag from the table at which she has been sitting all night. It is a hot summer night and the doors and french windows have all been open.
1 *What would you do if faced with this situation?*
2 *How would you record the incident?*
3 *What would you report to your manager?*

Recording lost property

In most establishments there are procedures for recording lost property. This usually covers personal property lost by customers, visitors or staff rather than property which may have been deliberately removed from the premises.

If someone reports they have lost an item it is usual for this to be recorded in a Lost Property Book. A page from one of these is shown on page 30.
- The information required should be recorded clearly and accurately. This information can then be used as a reference point for any property found on the premises.

- When recording lost property it is particularly important to take a contact address or telephone number so that the person can be contacted should the item/s be found.
- If you should find property it is your responsibility to report the find so that it can be returned to the appropriate person.
- In some organisations, found property is retained for a period of, for example, three months and then either returned to the person who reported it or sent to a charity shop.

LOST PROPERTY RECORD					
Date/time loss reported	Description of item lost	Where item lost	Lost by (name, address, tel. no.)	Item found (where, when, by whom)	Action taken

A page from a Lost Property Book

Securing storage areas

Throughout the building there will be areas designated as storage, whether for customers or staff. These areas can often be used by a variety of people in the course of a day, so security of the area and the contents are essential.

Storage areas, particularly those allocated for use by customers (such as secure lockers in hotels) are especially sensitive and can lead to a great deal of damage to the business if items from such areas are lost or go missing. Store rooms, refrigerators, freezers and cellars often contain a great deal of stock which constitutes some of the assets of the business; these areas must be protected from potential loss.

Some items can be easily removed from the premises and are therefore of particular concern.

- *Small items* such as linen, cutlery, crockery, food, wine, toiletries, etc. can be easily concealed in a carrier bag or package and removed without too much difficulty.

- *Larger items* such as equipment, food packages and computers can also be removed, but will generally need more thought and planning beforehand.
- *Valuables* such as jewellery, watches and money can be easily concealed and removed from the premises and are often more difficult to trace.

It is sometimes extremely difficult to make an area completely secure, especially as the premises are often host to a large variety of people. It is therefore important to minimise the risk as much as possible by following some fundamental guidelines.

Before we explore those guidelines, complete the exercise below. This will help you to identify areas which are not as secure as they could be. This may be due to a lost key, poor working practice or laziness on the part of the staff concerned.

Do this

- Draw up a list of all of the designated storage areas within your department and indicate whether they are secured storage areas (ie. lockable) or unsecured storage areas. Make sure you include every area in your list, including those made available for customers, staff and the storage of company property.
- Once you have drawn up the list, tick those areas which are kept secure at all times. Identify the gaps, then discuss with your colleagues ways of improving the security of these areas.

Securing access

By carrying out regular checks like those given in the example above, you could highlight the need for improvement and increase the security of your area.

The following points show how you might prevent unauthorised access to certain areas.
- Ensure access to storage areas is restricted to specific individuals. This will make it easier to trace any missing items and is likely to reduce the risks.
- Limit the number of duplicate and master keys and keep a record of all key holders. Limiting access to keys makes it easier to control the movement of items around the building.
- Never leave keys lying around or in locks: this is an open invitation to an opportunist thief.

MEMORY JOGGER

How could you ensure you secure the areas within your establishment where access if restricted?

- Never lend keys to other staff, contractors or visitors; especially master keys. If you have been issued with a master key, you have responsibility for the access to that particular storage area.
- Follow any organisational procedures regarding the reporting of lost keys. It may be necessary to trace the lost key or have a new lock fitted to ensure the security of the area.
- If you are working in a secure area, eg. a food store room, always lock the room when you are leaving, even if only for a few moments.

These guidelines are by no means exhaustive, but should help you maintain the security within your area of work and raise your awareness about the potential risks.

Do this

- Add your own ideas to the guidelines listed above, taking into account the list of storage areas you drew up earlier.
- Keep the list in a prominent position, such as your notice board or locker to remind you about the 'do's and don'ts' of effective security practice.

Dealing with suspicious individuals

Since you are working in the business of hospitality, there will inevitably and frequently be strangers within the building. As part of your job you should keep yourself alert to the presence of strangers in areas reserved for staff, ie. in the staff areas, offices and corridors. Non-staff may have a legitimate reason for being there: they may be visiting or delivering some material. On the other hand, they may have found their way in and be looking for opportunities to steal.

An individual may seem suspicious to you for a number of reasons. The following list will give you some pointers to potential problems, but remember that behaviour and situations may or may not indicate that an offence is taking place. An individual fitting any of these descriptions might be said to be acting suspiciously:

- someone wearing an incorrect uniform, or a uniform that is ill-fitting or worn incorrectly
- someone asking for directions to certain areas where you would not expect them to work; for example someone wearing kitchen whites and asking directions to a bedroom
- someone carrying company property in an area not open to them
- someone who appears lost or disorientated (remember that they *may* be innocent new employees)
- someone who just *looks* suspicious: perhaps they are wearing heavy clothing in summer, or carrying a large bag into the restaurant. Large bags or coats can be used to remove items from your premises
- someone who seems nervous, startled or worried, or is perspiring heavily
- a guest asking for details of someone else staying in the establishment. (In this case, it is better to pass on the enquiry rather than give out information to a stranger.)

Responding to a suspicious individual

If you see someone on the premises you do not recognise, or who looks out of place it is important that you:

1 challenge them politely: ask if you can help them, or direct them to the way out
2 report the presence of a stranger to your supervisor immediately.

Procedures for dealing with strangers will vary depending upon the establishment in which you work. In all cases, *do not put yourself at risk*. Do not approach the person if you feel uncomfortable or potentially threatened by them. Merely reporting any suspicions you have, whether it be about customers, staff or visitors can often be of great help to the security and long term health of the business.

MEMORY JOGGER

What would you need to do if you notice someone acting suspiciously

---

Do this

- Find out what procedures are laid down by your organisation for dealing with people acting in a suspicious manner.
- Discuss with your supervisor how you think you might challenge someone should you need to.

Case study

A member of staff has told you that she thinks someone has stolen her handbag from the staff locker area where she put it when she came into work. She said she placed the handbag in a locker, although she thinks it had a broken lock.

1 What would you do if faced with this situation?
2 How would you record the incident?
3 What would you report to your manager?

What have you learned	1	Why is it essential to maintain secure storage areas within your establishment?
	2	List five potential security risks within your own area.
	3	Why is it important you are aware of these risks?
	4	Which keys, property and areas should be secured from unauthorised access at all times?
	5	What should you ensure you do when leaving a secure area?
	6	What should you do if you see someone acting in a suspicious manner?
	7	How can you reduce the risk of items being taken from your own work area?
	8	Why is it important that you only give disclosable information to others?
	9	Why is it important to report any unusual/non routine incidents to the appropriate person?

Get ahead	1	Find out which foods are most at risk from bacteria.
	2	Carry out some research into the different types of bacteria which can cause food poisoning.
	3	Talk to your local Environmental Health Officer to find out about food poisoning statistics and the most common cause of the problem.
	4	Find out more about how the Food Hygiene Regulations relate specifically to food handlers.
	5	Find out about the *recovery position* in first aid. When would you need to use this? Why is it effective?
	6	Find out what immediate response you could give in the case of: burns and scalds, fainting, strokes and heart attacks.
	7	Talk to your security officers. Find out what kind of events they commonly deal with in your establishment.
	8	Invite a fire prevention officer to your establishment to talk about fire prevention and fire fighting in more detail.

Create and maintain effective working relationships

This chapter covers:

ELEMENT 1:   **Establish and maintain working relationships with other members of staff**

ELEMENT 2:   **Receive and assist visitors**

What you need to do

- Find out what your responsibilities are as an employee, in respect of health, safety, equal opportunities and confidentiality.
- Identify the working structures of your organisation so that you can seek and obtain advice and support in difficult or serious situations.
- Become familiar with the correct procedures and communication channels should an incident, breach of security or difficult situation occur with customers.
- Recognise the importance of passing important information on promptly and accurately within acceptable time scales to establish and maintain constructive working relationships.
- Identify why it is important to receive customers in a polite and professional manner and promote the products and services available within your organisation.

What you need to know

- What the company procedures are for dealing with awkward or aggressive customers.
- How to adapt methods of communication to suit the person you are dealing with.
- What the products and services of your organisation are.
- Why you should comply with equal opportunities.
- Where, when and from whom you should seek information.
- Why it is essential to be discreet when handling confidential information.
- What are the most appropriate methods of communication when proposing change.
- What systems are in place for dealing with emergencies, incidents and breaches of security.
- Why it is important to operate paging systems effectively.
- Why you should receive guests in a polite and professional manner.
- Why it is important to ensure when using any form of communication that the information is complete and accurate.

INTRODUCTION

In a service industry one of the most important parts of your job will be dealing with people. You may work within the same organisation with these people or they may be external eg. customers, suppliers, delivery people, maintenance personnel. The way that you deal with them will not only affect your relationship with them, but will also help them to form an impression of your company. Good people skills are not just about relationships, they are good for businesses too.

Dealing with people is a difficult skill because people are all individuals. You will need to develop many skills to deal with them. These skills relate to communication, team work and attitude as well as developing your knowledge about procedures, policies, legal requirements, structure, systems, products, services and the facilities of your organisation.

In order to maintain relationships there is a need to pay constant attention to behaviour. This is often easier with external customers, because you are aware of the relationship that you have with them as being service or product related. However we seldom consider what our colleagues or managers needs are. They are your customers too, they also need a product or a service from you as a team member. Teamwork is vital to the quality of the service and product being delivered by your organisation; everyone has a role to play.

ELEMENT 1:   Establish and maintain working relationships with other members of staff

---

WORKING WITHIN THE COMPANY STRUCTURE

Understanding your own job role is of great importance and in a well-structured company a written job description is usually provided. This normally contains the key tasks and duties that you should perform along with details of your responsibilities to your immediate supervisor and colleagues. In certain situations the details may not be written down and if that is the case it is important for you to have a discussion with your immediate supervisor to clarify your role and develop an agreed written job description.

Do this

- Obtain an organisational chart and identify your own job role within your department.
- Obtain a job description.
- Using the same chart, draw lines showing links that you have within your department.
- List the people that you have to deal with.
- Place all of the above in your portfolio of evidence.

TEAMWORK

What do you need from others to provide a service? What do others need from you to provide a product or a service? These questions are vitally important; as important as the relationships with external customers. In order to provide a quality product or service you will need the help of your colleagues. You must take the time to understand the pressures, priorities and schedules of other members of the staff.

For example, a waiter and a chef are reliant on each other to deliver the service to the customer. The waiter must ensure that the tables are laid out well with clean cutlery, the menu is explained and the order taken efficiently. The chef is then responsible for producing a meal to the desired quality and quantity within an acceptable time. In turn the chef relies on the kitchen porter to clean the pots, pans, kitchen area and maybe even do some basic vegetable preparation. As a team member you will be expected to play your part and the other members of the team to play theirs.

Other relationships within organisations are less apparent, such as the relationship between the housekeeping department and the kitchen, or between the reception and the kitchen. However these links still exist. Every job role within any organisation is interdependent on other departments. This relationship is based upon communication, which is the life blood of every organisation. The channels of communication will vary from organisation to organisation, however they all fall into two basic types, formal and informal.

Formal communication will take the form of standard operating procedures, organisational policy, procedures, legislative information, team briefings, memos, appraisal discussions, training sessions, coaching, telephone calls and letters.

MEMORY JOGGER

There are two channels of communication. What are they?

Informal communication usually occurs with one-to-one conversations, face-to-face, or in a brief telephone conversation.

Whether communication is informal or formal the importance of a constructive exchange cannot be overemphasised. Some of the benefits that flow from effective communication are that it:

● helps you to improve the service
● strengthens the team effort
● informs both internal and external customers of the latest situations.

Good communication is the key to successful businesses. Everyone needs to be kept informed. Well-informed people know what to expect and what is expected from them and understand what they can contribute to situations. Wherever you work good communication skills are necessary to achieve results. You need to know about appropriate communication channels, company structures, your role and the different situations that require contact with your line manager.

COMPANY STRUCTURES

Your own role and the role of others is formalised in the company structure. All companies, large or small, have some hierarchical structure. Within all organisations there are levels: these levels relate to job responsibilities. They indicate a line of command, for example as a chef your immediate line manager would be a *chef de partie*; in the absence of the *chef de partie* you would then report to the next level in line the Head Chef. In your organisation the structure may be simplified; there may only be a Head Chef and a Food and Beverage manager with overall responsibility for the food and beverage operation. The line of command is important to you because it indicates who you should contact if there is a situation that you cannot resolve.

A simple example of a hierarchical structure for a department might look like the example below:

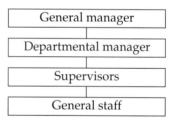

You can then add all other departments and the illustration might then becomes like this:

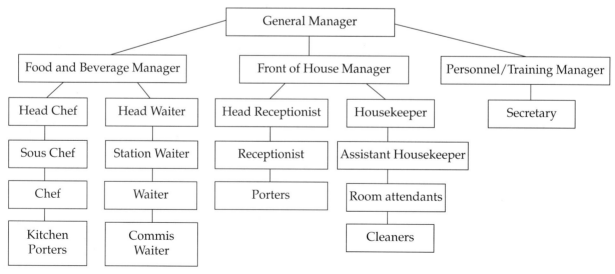

This structure when completed with all departments and names, forms a pyramid shape and is known as a pyramid structure. However more companies today are taking away the levels of management to produce a flatter structure, where the responsibilities are shared. In this type of organisation the communication channels are also likely to be easier because there are less levels involved and they may also rely more on informal communication rather than more formal memos and meetings.

Do this

Using the establishments organisational chart indicate:
● who you report to
● who requires a service from you and your department and who you require a service from
Make a list of these and then state whether communication is formal or informal.
Keep this information in your portfolio of evidence.

YOUR OWN ROLE WITHIN YOUR ORGANISATION

You will have certain responsibilities wherever you work. Some of these you will be aware of, others will affect you without you realising that they exist, these are laid down in legislation. The following is intended to raise your awareness of some of the legislation affecting you.

Common law rights and obligations

These rights and obligations affect both you and your employer, for the purpose of this unit a number of these have been identified that affect you. They are:
1 *A duty to serve* which in simple terms requires you to be ready and willing to work to your contract.
2 *A duty of competence* to carry out your job to a level expected within the organisation.
3 *A duty of good faith*; the most important part of this relates to confidentiality. You must ensure that nothing is done to damage your employer's business. Information relating to the company's profits and/or customers must not be divulged.

Essential knowledge

Do you know:
● what your role is within your organisation
● where you fit in
● what you should do
● which legislation affects you
● who your line managers are and how to contact them
● in what circumstances you should refer problems to line managers
● the most appropriate methods of communication?

Equal opportunities policies

You need to be aware what your responsibilities are under equal opportunities ruling. All companies should operate an equal opportunities policy. This relates to the equal opportunities available to every employee regardless of colour, gender, age, race, nationality, ethnic or national origin.

However, it is less well known that it is illegal for hotels and other similar establishments to discriminate against anyone with whom they do business. You will obviously be affected by this law and must serve people in these categories unless there are other reasons eg. if they are drunk or pose a threat to others.

You will also be affected by other legislation which is covered in other units relating to:
● health and safety at work which in general terms indicates that you must take reasonable care of yourself and others and that you must cooperate with your employer, so far as it is necessary to enable them to comply with any duty or requirements of the act or associated acts
● hygiene: relating to personal hygiene, wearing of appropriate clothing and to your working environment
● COSHH regulations: relating to the safe use and storage of hazardous material
● fire regulations
● reporting of accidents.

Summary
You need to be aware that your employer not only has a responsibility to you, but that you also have responsibilities to your employer, to internal and external customers.

MEMORY JOGGER

What action should be taken to ensure effective working relationships.

Do this

● Collect examples of the statutory law effecting you. Retain a copy of these documents in your portfolio.

COMMUNICATION SKILLS

People are the most important part of any business, whether they are internal colleagues, managers, external suppliers, visitors or customers. The way in which you communicate with them will make a difference to you, to them and to the business. It is important that when communicating with others you establish and build up a rapport.

The type of communication you use will depend upon who you are communicating with, what you need to communicate, why you need to communicate, and the speed with which you need to communicate - is it urgent or can it wait?

There are three general types of communication:
1 *verbal* – face-to-face; one-to-one; within a group; over the telephone
2 *non-verbal* – face-to-face or within a group
3 *written* – letters, notes, memos, fax, computer generated.

Face-to-face (verbal and non-verbal)
If communication is face-to-face, non-verbal communication will also play a part. First impressions are formed in the first few minutes of contact and are based largely upon non-verbal communication although stereotyping and prejudices will also play their part. Non-verbal communication is also known as body language. It is more likely to convey attitudes whereas verbal communication conveys information.

Body language accounts for nearly fifty-five percent of communication with people, so it is easy to see why it is so important to understand it, and also why some people prefer face-to-face contact, rather than using the telephone, computer or fax machine.

Body language can convey lots of messages; without realising it we all send out these messages. They are likely to be based upon:
● whether you like or think you might like the person you are dealing with
● how the person is reacting towards you.
● the situation in which the meeting takes place
☹ other situations which may have conditioned you.

The whole of the body is used when using non-verbal communication, hence the use of the name body language. The most expressive part of the body is the face, which can convey many different emotions and feelings. Facial expression can include the use of the eyes and mouth although the head is used as a whole when nodding to replace the spoken yes or no. The facial expressions used will be linked to other body movements and gestures which will also need to be read, but when you start to read body signals you must look at all of them to decide what they mean. Taking any one in isolation can be misleading.

MEMORY JOGGER

Body language conveys lots of messages. The way that we act towards others is likely to be effected by four reasons. What are they?

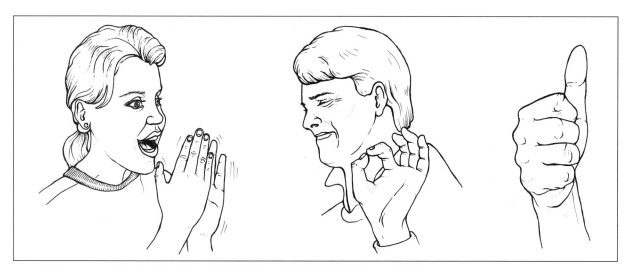

Face-to face communication: 'Isn't it exciting!', 'Everything's OK!', 'No worries!'

Do this

● Identify and list your own prejudices which may effect your body language and communication skills. (Recognising them will help to prevent you using them).

Verbal communication – telephone contact
The use of the telephone as a means of communication is very common. It is immediate and often enables you to talk with the person that you need straight away because you know where to contact them. Care needs to be taken when using the telephone because calls can often be overheard by others, so if the information is confidential, the telephone may not be the best method of communication.

When you use the telephone as part of your job you need to make sure that:
● you speak clearly
● you establish who you are, who you are speaking to and what the call is about
● you give clear information, taking notes if necessary

- that you take action on any points that you may have agreed during the conversation.

The organisation that you work for may also have certain procedures to follow when using the telephone, eg. how you should answer the telephone, how many rings the telephone makes before being answered, what you should say, how you should record the messages, when you need to pass the call on and how to pass the call on.

Do this

- Find out if your organisation has any laid down telephone procedures, if they do then obtain a copy for you portfolio of evidence. If they don't, write down what procedures you use and include examples of messages as well as a summary of how, when and why this method of communication was chosen.

Verbal communication difficulties When communicating with people there may be barriers. The sorts of common barriers that we encounter relate to language. Difficulties can be caused by dialects, jargon and accents. If you have to deal with people with language difficulties you will need to check that they have understood you and that you have understood them. This is achieved by using questions or gestures to confirm the level of understanding.

Emotions are conveyed in language by pitch, tone and volume. You will use a variety of skills to interpret and react to the person that you are dealing with. For example if you encounter someone who is annoyed or aggressive they will often use a raised voice. You must avoid shouting otherwise the situation is unlikely to calm down. You will also need to control your body language to avoid appearing to be a threat or being aggressive in return.

Written communication
Written communication has many forms: letter, memos, notes, computer generated information, facsimile messages and so on. When using writing as a method of communication you must ensure that:
- the style is appropriate to the reader
- it is clear who it is from, what it is about
- it is accurate, correctly worded and spelt.

It is also vital that all written communication is circulated only to the intended audience. It is therefore important to establish whether it is the most suitable method of communication and ensure that anyone who needs to see it does.

Confidential information needs to be handled discreetly and may require a combination of communication methods to ensure confidentiality is maintained.

Do this

- Prepare some examples of written communication to a variety of people within your organisation. You could include written material to suppliers, or other internal customers.

EFFECTIVE WORKING RELATIONSHIPS

Communication is a tool used to establish and maintain relationships with internal and external customers within an organisation. It is important to keep other people around you informed about what is going on, state what you need to deliver the product or service, and mention any problems you have encountered. By using communication effectively the quality of the product and/or service of your organisation can be maintained and improved.

Different organisations will use different methods of communication to achieve results. You need to demonstrate that you have taken appropriate opportunities to discuss work-related matters using the correct communication channels.

There are some simple rules that you need to follow in order to maintain effective working relationships. They are:
● always keep other people informed of the situation
● take care in selecting the method of communication. Consider what you want to say, the best method of communicating it and how you phrase the communication.
● always use the correct communication channels, based upon your organisation's structure.
● always deliver whatever you have promised to others promptly.

Case study

You have recently started to work in the a kitchen in a large hotel as a chef. You are working directly under a chef who has been at the hotel for many years. He is not particularly friendly and makes you work hard, which you do not particularly mind. However you begin to suspect that he is taking home food from the kitchen, in reasonably large quantities.
1 What should you do?
2 If he is taking the food, who should you report the matter to?
3 What do you see as the problems that you may encounter?
4 What might be the likely repercussions of your action?

COMMITMENT TO GET RESULTS

The success of any organisation is reliant on gaining the commitment of people who work within it. Establishing the role that each person has within the organisation, and appreciating how everyone fits together to form a team, is vital. As part of a team your individual contribution to the organisation, other team members and external customers, is all of fundamental importance to achieving results.

In addition to knowing your own job role, the role of others and the method of communication you will also need to know about the products, services, standards for service and organisational policies. In order to achieve this you will need to ensure that you obtain as much information as possible about the organisation where you work.

What have you learned

1 What is your role within the department and the organisation?
2 Who is your line manager?
3 What are the most appropriate methods of communication for the following: handling a disagreement; handling a conflict; dealing with a problem?
4 What are your responsibilities under equal opportunities legislation?
5 Why is it important to consult other people about changes?
6 When and how should you consult other people about changes?
7 Why it is important to be discreet when handling confidential information?
8 What different methods of communication do you use and when is it appropriate to use them?
9 Why do you need to adapt and use different approaches in different situations?
10 What are the three methods of communication ?
11 What percentage of our communications involves body language?

ELEMENT 2:   Receive and assist visitors

RECEIVE AND ASSIST VISITORS

Receiving visitors is one of the most important duties that you will perform for your organisation, although you may work behind the scenes. However you deal with these visitors, whether they are internal, external, expected or unexpected, it is essential that you should always maintain a degree of professionalism to maintain standards and ensure security.

The visitors impression of the organisation that you work for is created by the people as much as the environment. First impressions are considered to be the most important impressions that are left with us. Creating a good first impression is vital. Many companies have recognised the importance of creating a good impression and have developed detailed procedures for dealing with visitors.

Wherever you fit within the organisation, if a visitor arrives your should be able and willing to deal with them. The creators of Disneyland recognised this when they created their theme parks. They found that the most likely people to be asked directions were the staff keeping the parks tidy, these staff were given the same amount of knowledge about the parks as the information staff. Other companies have also recognised the importance of all their staff's skills.

Most of the time the service we give and receive is adequate. If the service falls below expected norms a complaint may be made, if you are lucky. From a complaint it is possible to learn a lot and improve the level of service. Compliments come from service that exceeds expectations and must therefore be exceptional: hence the fact that you are much more likely to receive letters of complaint than complimentary letters.

There are some simple rules that should always be followed to ensure that the service given to visitors fulfils both their needs and the needs of the organisation.

All visitors should be:
1   greeted promptly
2   the nature of their business established
3   directed to the appropriate people, products or services within the organisation promptly
4   any difficulties should be acknowledged and assistance sought from the most appropriate person.

There are different procedures for dealing with visitors which detail how you should greet customers and deal with them depending on where you work. An example of this might be whether, rather than simply giving directions to a customers, you should accompany them to their destination. This will help to maintain health, safety, security and confidentiality.

PROMOTING BUSINESS

It is important that you know about the products that your organisation offers. You should be aware of the products of each department, not just of your own. This offers you the opportunity to sell the products, services and facilities of your organisation, not simply your department. An example of this would be on reception where ideally the receptionist gives basic information about the facilities and then offers the customer the opportunity to book a wake-up call, breakfast, papers and a meal in the restaurant. This opportunity exists for all staff, who should be able to

---

MEMORY JOGGER

Why is it important to create a good first impression when receiving and assisting visitors.

promote the organisation's products and services. In order to do that you need to be able to describe what these products and services are. Equally important is the need to direct visitors or customers to the correct facility or person.

Essential knowledge

- You need to be familiar with your organisation's procedures.
- You should be able to promote the facilities of the organisation by being familiar with what your organisation has to offer.

Do this

Describe or obtain copies of the procedures your organisation has in place for:
- dealing with visitors
- routing visitors to other parts of the organisation
- dealing with emergencies, including aggressive customers
- promoting the facilities of the organisation.

Promoting the services and products is good for business. You should always recognise this when dealing with both internal and external customers. It is business that keeps everyone in employment at all levels and each department within the organisation. Knowing about the place where you work is good for business but it also has many benefits for you, the organisation and the customer.

For you:
- it makes you feel part of the organisation that you work in
- it allows you to act professionally
- it creates good team spirit.

For your organisation:
- it creates a good impression to customers
- it maintains security
- it is cost effective
- it promotes sales.

For the customer:
- it creates a good first impression
- the external customer is likely to return, the internal customer is likely to be more helpful towards you when you need some help, information or a product
- they are likely to return or contact you again.

Do this

- Write a description of the organisation's products and services. Include all departments.
- Find out what the procedure is for evacuation of external customers if there is a fire where you work.

COMMUNICATION

Choosing the most appropriate method of communication is very important. When dealing with any person that you come into contact with, you need to chose the right method of communication, suited to the needs of that person. You will need to take into account:
- who they are
- what they want
- if they have any special needs eg. if they are foreign speaking, hearing impaired, or in a wheelchair where access could be a problem.

Routine enquiries

Most of the time the enquiries that you will be dealing with will be routine, those which form most of your working contact with people. One example of this would be routing people to other parts of the organisation. For this you will clearly need to know the layout of your place of work and the best way to reach different areas. You must also be aware of any routing policies that your organisation may have. For example if someone asked if Mr Smith was in room 36 what should you do? This particular example would also be affected by the need to protect confidential information and there is usually a company policy covering this. Confidentiality is very important; you must be careful not to divulge private information. If in doubt you should always check with a supervisor.

Complex enquiries

You are likely to have to deal with people in many complex situations; angry, upset, aggressive, drunk or distressed due to an emergency. There may be procedures for dealing with problem situations eg. aggressive customers or emergency situations. You need to check whether there are such procedures in place and what the procedure or policy states you should do. Where they do not exist the following suggestions should provide some guidance:

● always try to stay calm
● try to move the angry customer away to a quiet area
● if they are very angry, let them have their say, this time will allow you to think
● try to identify what their needs are
● don't argue: speak softly – this will have several effects. Firstly it is likely to calm them down and secondly it is more difficult to argue with someone when they are speaking softly.
● acknowledge your own difficulties as quickly as possible and seek help from the most appropriate person within the organisation.

Eventually the customer usually runs out of steam. Try to judge if you can deal with the customer or if you require assistance. It is important to establish this early on, otherwise the customers will have to explain the situation all over again, which is likely to make them even more angry or distressed.

Dealing with emergencies requires some basic knowledge of the company procedures. In the case of emergencies procedures and policies often exist.

Do this

Find out if there are procedures for the following:
● fire
● suspicious packages
● bomb alert
● unknown visitors
● dealing with aggressive visitors.

Essential knowledge

You need to know what your own responsibilities are for the following examples:
● What do you do if you find a package?
● What must you do if there is a fire or a fire alarm?
● Why you should challenge people you find wandering around your establishment?
● Who you should contact?
● When and how can you contact someone else when you are in a in difficult situation?
● What are your organisation's products and services?

PAGING SYSTEMS

Paging systems are used in many large organisations where people have to be contacted but there is no telephone extension near to where they are working. There are two types of paging systems used:

● an electronic bleep that simply identifies that the person is required and should report back to a central point of contact, often reception
● an audible message is transmitted using strategically placed speakers usually used in reception areas of public rooms.

HEALTH, SAFETY AND SECURITY

Security is becoming an increasing problem for organisations. With fewer people employed large areas are now left unattended.

Where a workplace is visited by a large number of people it is very difficult to control access. Many catering organisations such as hotels have a large number of exits, so the maintenance of security is compounded again. It is therefore important that any person entering your place of work is challenged about why they are there and what they want.

You should make sure that you are familiar with any laid down procedures, since in any of these circumstances you need to react quickly. Being familiar with the procedures helps because you do not have to think of a solution. Most of the time you will be able to refer the matter to the appropriate line manager. However, there may be occasions when that person is not available. In this situation your knowledge of the company structure is vital, so that you can contact the next most appropriate person.

DEALING WITH EMERGENCIES

There are a few basic steps that you should try to follow in any emergency situation.
1   Do not panic, try to stay calm.
2   Try to think clearly about the situation. If you feel it is beyond your control, contact someone who can help quickly, before the situation gets out of hand.
3   Always try to speak calmly, to avoid panic in others.
4   Try to use the procedures that your organisation has developed – they are there to help.

The best preparation is *knowledge*, so you need to make sure that you know your job well and that you understand your role, your responsibilities and how they fit in to other people's.

Case study

You are working in the kitchen of a large hotel. Two men arrive in overalls and say that they have come to repair the refrigerators, asking you where they are located. You take them over to the fridges and they start work, by removing the front doors from both fridges. Each workman leaves the kitchen carrying a door. They do not return to complete the work and to everyone's amazement, it appears that they have stolen the doors. (This is based upon a true situation!)

1   What should you have done?
2   Whom might you have contacted to verify their orders?
3   What can you learn from this?
4   If you were going to write a procedure for dealing with visitors turning up unexpectedly, what would you include in it?

1   What are the systems for security in place within your organisation?
2   What are the procedures for dealing with: aggressive visitors; emergencies?
3   What paging systems are there and when might you use them?
4   Why is it important to allocate roles and responsibilities clearly via the organisational structure?
5   What products and services does your organisation have available?
6   What are your responsibilities for dealing with visitors?
7   What are your responsibilities in complying with equal opportunities in relation to visitors?
8   What are the systems in operation in your establishment to maintain security?

Get ahead

1   Find out if there are other legislative laws affecting your job role.
2   Find out what legal problems could occur if you did not handle an incident correctly.
3   Find out the names of all the companies that carry out work for your establishment and make a list including the internal contact.
4   Look at the other units in this book and see what evidence or additional material they could provide for this unit.

Clean food production areas, equipment and utensils

This chapter covers:
ELEMENT 1:   **Clean food production areas**
ELEMENT 2:   **Clean food production equipment**
ELEMENT 3:   **Clean food production utensils**

What you need to do

- Check that sinks, wash basins, drains, gullies, traps and overflows are clean, free-flowing and satisfy food hygiene regulations. Clean them as necessary.
- Check that floors and walls are clean and satisfy health, safety and food hygiene regulations. Clean them as necessary.
- Check that all food production equipment is turned off and dismantled before cleaning.
- Clean food production equipment correctly then store it appropriately.
- Check that shelving, cupboards and drawers are clean and tidy, and satisfy health, safety and hygiene regulations. Clean them as necessary.
- Clean food production utensils correctly; check that they are dry, clean, free from damage and then store them appropriately.
- Leave any cleaning equipment used in a clean and tidy state and stored correctly.
- Handle and dispose of waste correctly.
- Report any problems with cleaning equipment, waste containers and general maintenance.

What you need to know

- The reasons for cleaning.
- How to plan your time efficiently, taking care of priorities and any laid down procedures.
- Why equipment is turned off and dismantled before cleaning.
- How to deal with unexpected situations.
- Why waste must be handled and disposed of correctly.
- Which type of cleaning equipment and materials to use in food production areas and on equipment and utensils.
- The current legislation regarding safe practices when cleaning.

WHAT IS *CLEANING*?

Cleaning is the removal of all food residues and any dirt or grease that may have become attached to work surfaces, equipment and utensils during the preparation and cooking of food.

To clean effectively, we need to use *energy*. This can be in the form of:

1. *physical energy*. For example: scrubbing by hand or mechanical equipment. This removes any food debris which may have remained on cooking equipment or utensils
2. *heat energy (thermal)*. For example: hot water or steam. This helps to melt grease and fat, making it easier to scrub clean. Heat energy can also be used to destroy bacteria. This will only happen when the temperature is above 82 °C (180 °F)

MEMORY JOGGER

At what temperature does water destroy bacteria?

MEMORY JOGGER

What is
1 A detergent
2 A disinfectant
3 A steriliser
4 A sanitiser?

MEMORY JOGGER

What is the difference between a disinfectant and a steriliser?

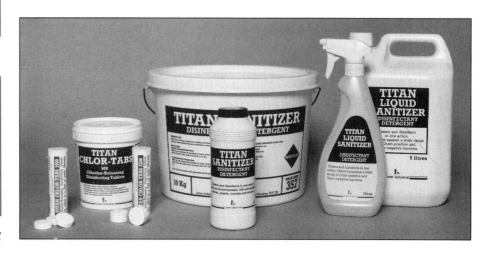

Chemicals used for cleaning

3 *chemical energy.* For example: the use of detergents and disinfectants, Note the following:
- a *detergent* will dissolve grease and fat but will not kill bacteria
- a *disinfectant* removes infection (reduces bacteria to a safe level) but will not dissolve fats
- a *steriliser* will kill all living micro-organisms
- a special cleaning product called a *sanitiser* combines the effects of both detergent and disinfectant.

THE REASONS FOR CLEANING

All food handlers, like doctors, have a *legal and a moral responsibility* to their customers. It is up to you to prevent outbreaks of food poisoning. The reasons we clean are:
- to comply with the law
- to remove any food debris on which bacteria may grow. This will reduce the risk of food poisoning
- to enable disinfectants to be effective on work and equipment surfaces
- to remove any food which may attract food pests, eg. insects, rodents, birds and domestic pets
- to reduce the contamination of food by foreign matter, eg. dust, flaking paint, grease from mechanical equipment
- to make the area in which you are working a pleasant and safe place
- to make a favourable impression on customers.

PLANNING YOUR TIME

In order to be effective and efficient you need to consider the best method of working, so that cleaning is carried out in a methodical and systematic way.
- Identify the areas, equipment or utensils that you will be required to clean and when they need to be ready to use again.
- Plan ahead: have all your cleaning equipment and materials ready.
- *Clean as you go* is the basic motto, but always check the most appropriate time to clean.
- Mop up spillages immediately.
- Remember that stoves and floors should be cleaned immediately before and after every service.
- Clean and wipe down walls, shelves, cupboards and drawers regularly.
- Wash out drains and gullies every day.
- Wipe down sinks and hand basins after using them.
- Check cleaning schedules for the best times to clean heavy equipment.

Replace worn out parts of equipment regularly

It is always easier to clean equipment and dirty utensils immediately after using them. If you leave it too long, the food debris dries up and becomes more difficult to remove. It also makes your area look dirty, unprofessional and provides an open invitation to pests, bacteria and cross-contamination.

HEALTH, SAFETY AND HYGIENE

Make sure that you are familiar with the general points given in Unit NG1 (pages 2–8 and 15–27) and Unit 2ND22 (pages 97–110).

Precautions when using cleaning chemicals

● Always read and follow the instructions carefully. Pay attention to first aid procedures.
● Use protective clothing, eg. gloves, when handling and using chemicals as some products are highly dangerous when in direct contact with human tissue. Refer to the COSHH regulations (*Control of Substances Hazardous to Health*). Ask your supervisor to supply you with this information.
● Ensure that you use the correct product for the appropriate job, eg. do not use chlorine bleach on food contact surfaces because it will taint and may contaminate the food.
● Always keep cleaning products in their own containers and make sure they are clearly labelled. Store them in a place which is not used for food storage.
● *Never* put cleaning chemicals into a food container or food into a chemical container.
● Remember that it is dangerous to mix cleaning chemicals. They may react and give off toxic fumes or they may become ineffective.
● If chemical cleaners require diluting, only do so immediately prior to use; otherwise they may lose their active qualities and become stagnant solutions which may harbour bacteria.
● Always use the correct concentration: if you do not dilute chemical cleaners enough the liquid may be difficult to rinse off and will lead to food contamination; if you dilute them too much they will be ineffective.
● Do not dispose of cleaning solutions in food preparation sinks.
● Clean the cleaning equipment itself (eg. brushes and cloths) after use. Store them away from food in a well-ventilated area to allow them to dry.

Unexpected situations/problems

If you notice any damage to the cleaning equipment, or if there is insufficient protective clothing or materials, report it immediately to your supervisor. You must also report any problems with chemicals regarding their storage. If you are in any doubt about how to use a particular chemical ask to be trained. It is now a legal requirement that all staff using chemicals are properly trained (COSHH).

If food becomes contaminated with a cleaning chemical it must be discarded immediately.

Any spillages of concentrated cleaning chemicals must be carefully diluted and mopped up because they seriously damage surfaces and equipment.

Do this

● Check which cleaning chemicals are used in your kitchen. Read their instructions.
● Note where they are stored.
● Find out what protective clothing/equipment, if any, you need to use when applying each product.
● Write a brief report to your manager on any problems you notice with cleaning materials, waste containers or general maintenance.

Case study

You are making 15 litres of potato soup for a special lunch party, you have added all the ingredients to the basic stock and seasoned it, all it needs to do is come to the boil, simmer for 20 minutes and it will be ready to liquidise. Just as the soup is coming to the boil it starts to froth and it then boils over creating a terrible mess. The head chef comes over and asks you to taste the soup. You taste it and immediately notice the horrible taste of soap! The head chef then points to the salt container – it is full of white detergent powder.

1   What safety precautions were neglected?
2   Who is responsible for preventing the contamination of food?
3   What can be done to prevent this sort of contamination?

ELEMENT 1:   Clean food production areas

Areas to be cleaned will include:
- *metal tables, sinks and panelling.* Use a non-abrasive cloth and cleaner. Clean with a detergent and disinfectant, or a sanitiser, then rinse with hot water. Avoid using chlorine bleach or scented disinfectants on food-contact surfaces. Make sure that sinks and hand-basins are clean and free-flowing.
- *wall tiles.* Clean with a detergent and disinfectant, or a sanitiser. Pay special attention to walls around stoves, bins and preparation areas.
- *painted surfaces.* Use a non-abrasive cloth and cleaner. Clean with a detergent and disinfectant, or a sanitiser.
- *floor tiles, vinyl, linoleum floor coverings.* Use a strong degreaser (a detergent) and disinfectant. Ensure that drains, gullies, traps and overflows are clean and free-flowing. While cleaning floors, place an obvious warning sign in the area, indicating that the floor is wet, then dry floors after cleaning to avoid accidents.
- *glass.* Use detergent or specialised products. Dry with a clean, soft cloth.
- *laminated surfaces (formica).* Clean with a detergent and disinfectant, or a sanitiser. Make sure that shelving, cupboards and drawers are clean and tidy.

> **MEMORY JOGGER**
>
> What should you use to clean floors and what additional precautions should you take?

A cleaning trolley carrying equipment and warning signs

REMOVING WASTE

Waste includes all packaging, food trimmings and any leftover food. Waste bins are a perfect environment for promoting the growth of bacteria and need to be treated as a major source of contamination. *Never use a waste bin for storing food* and never use food storage containers (like flour bins) as waste bins.

Follow the guidelines given below:
- empty bins regularly: do not wait until they are full, especially when they contain moist food debris as this will attract pests and create bad odours
- take special care after handling rubbish bins and waste food: always wash your hands
- waste bins, their lids and surrounding areas must be thoroughly cleaned. Use a strong detergent and disinfectant
- store waste in the correct designated areas. These should be away from food preparation areas, corridors and fire exits.

<table>
<tr><td>

MEMORY JOGGER

What is the correct way to remove waste?
</td></tr>
</table>

Essential knowledge

When cleaning food production areas, waste must be handled and disposed of correctly in order to:
- prevent accidents
- prevent infection from waste
- avoid creating a fire hazard
- prevent pest infestation
- avoid pollution of the environment
- comply with the law.

Do this

With guidance from your supervisor, clean:
- metal sinks (checking that they are free-flowing)
- wall tiles (including those around stoves, bins and preparations areas)
- glass surfaces
- the kitchen floor (checking that drains, gullies, traps and overflows are clean and free-flowing
- any glass surfaces in the kitchen.

What have you learned

1 Why is it important to handle and dispose of waste correctly when cleaning food production areas?
2 What must you take into account when planning your cleaning?
3 What are the four types of chemicals commonly used for cleaning food production areas?
4 When might you need to use protective clothing when cleaning?

ELEMENT 2: Clean food production equipment

Before cleaning

Always make sure that the food production equipment is correctly turned off and dismantled before cleaning. After you have cleaned it, make sure that all the parts are dry and then carefully reassemble the equipment.

See also Unit 2ND17, Cleaning cutting equipment, pages 90–94

Essential knowledge

All equipment must be turned off and dismantled before cleaning in order to:
● avoid injury to the person cleaning the machine
● ensure that all the relevant parts are thoroughly cleaned
● ensure that the machine works efficiently
● conserve energy.

CLEANING DIFFERENT TYPES OF EQUIPMENT

Ovens

● Use specialised chemicals such as heavy-duty oven cleaners. Pay attention to instructions and take appropriate safety precautions.
● As oven cleaners are highly toxic, ensure that the oven is *thoroughly rinsed* after cleaning.

Griddles or grills and salamanders

● Use specialised chemicals designed to remove carbon (burnt food residues).
● Pay attention to instructions on the packaging and take appropriate safety precautions.

Hobs and range

● Refer to the cleaning manual for the particular equipment you are using, ie. metal or ceramic, electric or gas-fuelled hobs.
● Ensure that the cooking equipment is isolated from the mains supply before cleaning.
● Correctly reassemble equipment after cleaning and check that it is operational again.

Fryers

Refer to the cleaning manual and use a special degreaser. Take appropriate safety precautions.
1 Ensure that the electricity or gas burner and pilot are turned off.
2 Drain out the oil, using a filter, when the oil is warm; *never when it is hot*.
3 Always drain into a dry, clean container which is large enough to hold the oil easily.
4 Remove the bottom strainer from the fryer and wash this separately with a detergent/degreaser. Dry thoroughly.
5 Clean out any loose scraps of burnt food debris from the fryer. Wash the inside of the pan using a strong detergent/degreaser. Rinse well and dry thoroughly.
6 Clean the lid, the outside of the fryer and the surrounding area, checking for oil spillages.
7 See that the drain tap is closed, and then refill the fryer with clean, strained or new oil.
8 When not in use, close the lid of the fryer, and check that all gas taps are closed and that the mains switch is in the *off* position.

A deep fat fryer

Bain maries or hotplates

● *Dry bain maries.* isolate dry bain maries and hotplates before cleaning and allow to cool. Remove any food debris and clean with detergent and a damp cloth.

● *Wet bain maries*: drain and clean these with a detergent, then rinse them and refill with fresh water.

Refrigerators, freezers and cold rooms

This storage equipment needs special attention.
● Clean the inside walls and floors frequently.
● Mop up any spillages immediately, as they may cause serious cross-contamination.
● Use a detergent and disinfectant which will not taint the food. Rinse very well with hot water.
● Defrost the cooling element regularly. This will prevent a build-up of ice and make the equipment easier to clean.
● Plan your cleaning time carefully to prevent the internal temperature of the equipment rising for too long.

Food processors

For information about cleaning food processors, see Unit 2ND17, *Cleaning cutting equipment*, pages 92–94.

Do this

With guidance from your supervisor, clean:
● ovens, hobs and ranges
● grilling equipment, eg. grill or salamander.
● fryers
● dry and wet bain maries
● refrigerators and freezers.

What have you learned

1 Why is it important to handle and dispose of waste correctly when cleaning food production utensils?
2 Why would you need to use specialised chemicals when cleaning grills and salamanders?
3 How would you clean a dry bain mairie?
4 Why must you always turn off and dismantle equipment before cleaning?
5 Why should you regularly defrost the cooling element of a freezer?

ELEMENT 3: Clean food production utensils

All food production utensils need to be kept very clean as they are a major cause of cross-contamination. Make sure they are thoroughly dry before storing them after cleaning.

Stainless steel utensils

This category includes pots, pans and whisks. Clean the utensils with detergents and hot water above 82 °C (180 °F).

Sieves, colanders and strainers may need to be soaked in cold water to loosen the food. The wire mesh of sieves and strainers needs to be thoroughly dried to avoid rust.

Coated metal utensils

Enamel is often used to coat metal utensils, and this can chip very easily. Use a brush or sponge for cleaning, and avoid using abrasive materials and cleaners.

Wood utensils

This category includes spoons and rolling pins. Thoroughly wash these with a detergent and hot water and make sure they are absolutely dry before storing them. Any wooden utensils which have cracks or splinters must be discarded.

Essential knowledge

When cleaning food production utensils, waste must be correctly handled and disposed of in order to:
- prevent accidents
- prevent risk of fire
- prevent contamination of food and food areas
- comply with the law.

Plastic utensils

This category includes spoons, bowls and chopping boards. Thoroughly wash with detergent and a sanitiser, then rinse with hot water (82 °C/180 °F). Take special care when cleaning plastics that cannot withstand extreme temperatures (check the manufacturer's instructions).

Glasswashers offer a time-saving alternative

Porcelain, earthenware and glass utensils

This category includes bowls and service dishes. Thoroughly wash with detergent and hot water (82 °C/180 °F). Any cracked or chipped utensils must be discarded because they can harbour germs and cause accidents. *Never leave glass items in a full sink.*

MEMORY
JOGGER

What precautions should you take when cleaning knives?

Small utensils

These need to be washed with a detergent and hot water (82 °C/180 °F). Make sure that you wash the handles. Knives should be thoroughly cleaned after each use and never left in a full sink. Knives, vegetable peelers and other sharp-edged utensils such as graters need to cleaned and dried carefully to avoid accidents.

Tin openers

These need to cleaned after *every* use. Use a brush with detergent and hot water (82 °C/180 °F), taking care not to cut yourself on the sharp edge.

Do this

With guidance from your supervisor, clean a few articles from each of the following categories:
- stainless steel sieves and colanders
- enamel utensils (if used)
- plastic chopping boards
- porcelain or earthenware service dishes
- knives

What have you learned

1 Why must waste be correctly disposed of when cleaning food production utensils?
2 Why should you never leave glass items in a sink?
3 Why should you check the manufacturer's instructions before cleaning plastic utensils?
4 State five precautions that must be observed when using cleaning chemicals.
5 What temperature does water need to reach in order to disinfect?

Get ahead

1 Read through the cleaning schedule in your kitchen and discuss the planning of it with your supervisor.
2 Find out exactly how the chemicals in a detergent work.
3 Ask your supervisor for permission to take swab tests from various areas in the kitchen and grow your own colonies of bacteria in a petri dish.
4 Visit a laboratory where food samples from production kitchens are checked.
5 Find out which cleaning agents use an acid base to clean and which use an alkali base.
6 Call your cleaning chemical supplier or the Department of Health for more information on *The Care of Substances Hazardous to Health*.

Maintain and handle knives

This chapter covers:
ELEMENT 1:   **Maintain knives**
ELEMENT 2:   **Handle knives**

What you need to do

- Clean and sharpen knives for use and clean after use according to laid down procedures and satisfying food hygiene regulations.
- Handle and store knives in accordance with laid down procedures.
- Show mastery of basic knife skills.

What you need to know

- Why knives should be kept sharp.
- The main contamination threats when using knives.
- Why it is important to keep preparation and production areas and equipment clean and hygienic.
- Why knives should be handled correctly.
- The correct use for each knife.
- How to hold and handle your knives correctly and efficiently.

INTRODUCTION

It is very important that you learn to handle, maintain and care for your knives from the beginning of your training as a chef. Given time and practice they will become an extension of your hands.

You will also need to learn how to select the correct knife for the job in hand, such as a filleting knife for filleting fish. During your training you may well come across a great number of cutting, shredding and chopping machines, but none of these can produce the same fine quality of work you will be able to achieve with a sharp knife.

Acquiring these skills takes time and practice. There are certain rules you need to learn before starting to work with knives:
1 always use the knife best suited to the job
2 maintain your knives in a clean and sharp condition
3 handle all knives safely and in a methodical manner
4 once you have chosen the knives you are going to use, place them flat on the work surface with the blade facing inwards
5 never try to catch a knife if it is falling to the floor
6 never leave knives in a sink
7 only ever have one knife on the chopping board at any one time
8 never leave knives on the edge of the table or board
9 never allow knives to become hidden under food items.

Why are these rules important?

Some of these rules will have struck you as common sense, but all of them are commonly broken during training.

1 Choose the correct knife
Failure to do this can be dangerous for a number of reasons, but two of the main ones are as follows:

● if the knife is too large you will not have adequate control over it and you are therefore more likely to have an accident
● if you chose a knife with a rigid blade when you need a flexible blade you will not be able to work as quickly or as efficiently as possible, and you may even have an accident.

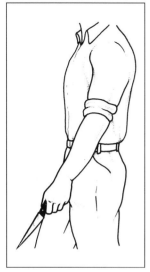

MEMORY JOGGER

Why is it necessary to choose the correct size and type of knife as well as making sure it is sharp

The correct way to carry a knife

MEMORY JOGGER

What is the possible outcome if a knife is left in a sink of soapy water?

Never leave knives in a sink

2 Keep knives clean and sharp
You must always keep your knives *clean* because:
● you have less control over dirty, greasy or wet knives
● cutting raw and cooked produce with the same unwashed knife can cause cross-contamination. Always work hygienically.

You must always keep knives *sharp* because:
● a blunt knife requires more pressure to allow it to cut through a food item; this extra pressure can cause loss of control and therefore accidents
● a blunt knife will take longer than a sharp knife to complete a task and the finished result will not be as neat and accurate as when done with a sharp knife.

3 Handle knives safely and methodically
Careless handling of knives causes accidents.
● Carry knives carefully, by holding the handle, pointing the knife downwards towards the floor with the sharp edge pointing behind you. Keep it slightly away from the body.
● Never transport knives around the kitchen by placing them on a board and then carrying the board. They could easily fall off and cause an accident.
● Never threaten any one with a chef's knife (even in jest) however small its blade may be.

4 Place knives on the workbench carefully
Always place knives flat on the worksurface to avoid the following situations:
● if you allow a knife to stand on the board or work surface with the sharp side of the blade standing upwards someone may accidentally lean on it and cut themselves
● if the blade is left facing outwards from the board and you (or a colleague) then wipe the work area, you may cut yourself.

5 Never try to catch a falling knife
You must never try to save a falling knife, as it is very easy to mistime your catch, so that the blade runs through the palm of your hand. If you drop a knife, allow it to fall, keeping all of your limbs beyond reach.

6 Never leave knives in a sink
Leaving a knife in a sink is often considered to be one of the worst crimes you can commit when learning to handle knives, as it generally results in an accident to someone else rather than to you. Remember that knives in dirty water or full sinks are very difficult to spot.

7 Never place more than one knife on the chopping board
If you leave any knives other than the one you are using on the chopping board you could catch the other knife with the one you are using; this could result in damage to both knives or an injury to yourself.

8 Place knives on tables with care
You should always keep knives away from the edge of the table as they can easily be knocked off or catch someone walking by who is unable to see them.

9 Keep knives obvious
Do not allow knives to become hidden under food items as there is the same risk of accidental cuts as for *leaving knives in a sink* (Point 6 above).

Essential
knowledge

Knives should always be kept sharp in order to:
● maintain efficiency within food preparation
● keep pressure to a minimum when cutting
● complete tasks more quickly
● avoid risk of accident.

ELEMENT 1:   Maintain knives

SHARPENING KNIVES

The most traditional method of maintaining a sharp edge on a knife is by using a steel. Sharpening a knife can be a dangerous exercise if not done with care.

Read through the following instructions then practise with your knife, referring back to the text when necessary. *Do not try to sharpen a knife whilst reading the text as this could be dangerous.*

1   Select a steel and the knife you wish to sharpen.
2   Hold the steel in one hand with its point away from you and pointing slightly upwards.
3   Holding the knife firmly in the other hand, start by placing the hilt of the blade close to the steel.
4   Angle the knife at approximately 18° then firmly draw the blade across the steel.
5   Repeat this process by placing the knife on the underside of the steel.
6   Repeat Steps 4 and 5 several times.
7   To test for sharpness, carefully and gently draw your finger over the blade. It should feel slightly abrasive.
8   Now wash the knife to remove any filings that might be on the blade.

Sharpen your knife each time you come to use it or if it goes dull during use.

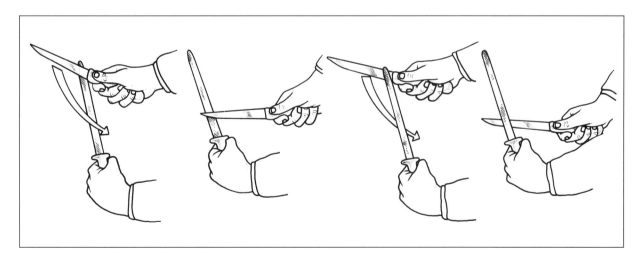

Sharpening a knife

Once a knife cannot be kept sharp by the use of a steel it should be re-ground professionally. There are both electric and manually operated table top grinding wheels available. This will replace the 'edge' on the knife which has been lost.

Knives should always be handled correctly in order to:
● avoid accidents to people
● avoid accidents to food items
● maintain a safe and secure work area
● obtain the required effect when cutting, chopping and slicing.

KNIFE SAFETY

Carrying knives

Carrying knives around the kitchen can be very dangerous. They should be carried with the point aimed downwards, held slightly away from the body, and with the sharp edge of the blade facing backwards.

You should *never* carry a knife with the point facing in front of you as someone could easily be hurt. Nor should you carry knives around on chopping boards as they may well slip off while you are carrying the board.

Maintaining knives

Good maintenance of your knives is essential for many reasons, from health and safety aspects to prolonging the life of your equipment. The following points need to be considered when maintaining knives:
● always keep knives clean, as you may be using them on both cooked and raw foods
● make sure the handles of knives are clean: if they are greasy they could cause the knife to slip during use
● always wash knives in hot water with detergent and then rinse them well
● when drying your knives, always make sure that the sharp side of the blade is facing away from you and that your fingers are not over the cutting edge
● store the clean knives safely by placing them back into their carrying wallet or a case specially adapted to hold them in individual compartments.

Never just throw your knives into a box, drawer or locker. They should always be placed into some form of compartmental holder to prevent you having an accident while searching for a particular knife. Searching through a pile of knives for the one that you want is also time wasting.

HEALTH, SAFETY AND HYGIENE

Make sure that you are familiar with the general points given in Unit NG1 (pages 2–33). Pay special attention to the sections on cross-contamination from raw and cooked foods using cutting implements (both mechanical and hand-held).

Cross-contamination is the transfer of harmful bacteria from one contaminated surface to another. The knife is an ideal vehicle in the transfer train due to its versatility. It is therefore essential for health, hygiene and safety reasons to methodically wash and clean each knife after use and immediately before starting a new task. Particular attention must be paid to cleanliness when using knives to work on first raw, then cooked foods, or from one type of food item to another.

Remember that the surface of the knife may appear clean to the naked eye but may actually be holding bacteria (evident under a microscope). These bacteria will be transferred to the next surface you cut. Always use a bactericidal detergent or sanitiser when cleaning knives and use a fresh, disposable wipe to dry them. Dispose of the wipe immediately after use.

Knives in a carrying case

The risks of cross-contamination will only be minimised by constant vigilance in your approach.

Do this

- Find an example of each of the knives and cutting implements listed on pages 61–63.
- Watch your chef using a boning knife. Notice how he or she holds the knife and what safety precautions are taken.
- List the reasons why you must always keep your knives sharp.
- Watch your supervisor chopping vegetables. Which knife does he or she use? What techniques does he or she use?
- Watch your supervisor cleaning a knife after use. What chemicals and materials does he or she use?

UNEXPECTED SITUATIONS

Reporting of accidents

All accidents should be reported to your immediate supervisor and recorded in the Accident Book which should be provided by the organisation. The reporting process is extremely important as accidents can become the subject of legal proceedings which can take several years to settle. It is in the interests of all that full and accurate details of how the accident occurred, the nature of the injury and the action taken are recorded in as much detail as possible.

If someone is cut by a knife, first establish the severity of the cut.

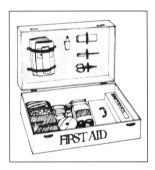

First aid kit

For a minor wound:

1 clean the wound (under running water or with a swab) then dry it gently
2 press a swab or dressing against the wound and raise the injured part to slow the flow of blood (where possible)
3 look after the injured person, keeping them calm, warm and as comfortable as possible
4 contact your first aider.

For a major wound:

1 *place a dressing over the wound* (large enough to cover the area easily)
2 *bandage over the dressing,* tying it firmly enough to control the bleeding but not so tightly that it affects circulation
3 *call for urgent medical help.* This might include calling both your own first aider and an ambulance.

Remember:
- a wound more than 1.75 cm ($\frac{1}{2}$ in) in length may need stitching in hospital
- blood can carry the HIV virus (which causes AIDS) and hepatitis. Cover any cuts or grazes on your own hands with a waterproof dressing before attending to a wound, and always wash your own hands before and after treating wounds.

Case study

During a busy service a commis chef is jointing some roast ducks. He stops to sharpen his knife with a steel. Whilst sharpening the knife it slips out of his hand and cuts his thumb on the steel hand. The commis picks up the knife which has duck fat all over the handle. Looking down at his finger he sees what looks like a deep cut.
1 *What should the commis do first?*
2 *Why should the commis report the accident?*
3 *How could the commis have prevented the accident in the first place?*

ELEMENT 2:   Handle knives

RANGE OF KNIVES

Each knife is produced to perform a particular function. The list given over the next two pages illustrates the types of knives and equipment you should be familiar with, together with the uses of each.

Steel
This is used to sharpen knives. A good steel should have a safety guard.

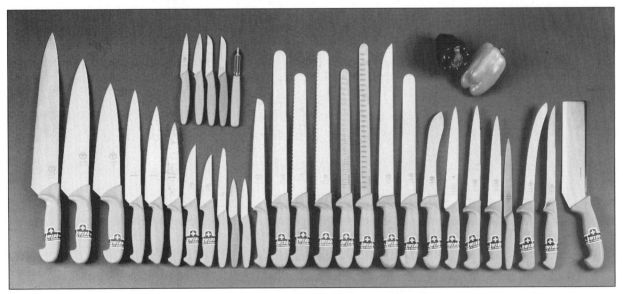

From top left: serrated parer; broad serrated parer; vegetable prep knife; vegetable prep knife; peeler
From bottom left: cook's knife (heavy 12" blade); cook's knife (heavy 10" blade); cook's knife (heavy 8½" blade); cook's knife (light 8½" blade); cook's knife (light 7½" blade); cook's knife (light 6½" blade); vegetable knife (heavy duty 5" blade); vegetable knife (heavy duty 4" blade); multi-purpose knife; broad parer; parer; bread knife; roast beef slicer; 10" slicer; 12" slicer: 10" salmon slicer; 12" salmon slicer; slicer with semi-flexible blade; roast beef slicer; fillet knife with curled rigid blade; meat fillet knife; 8" fillet knife; 7" fillet knife; 6" fish fillet knife; 8" fish fillet knife (curved blade); 8" fish fillet knife (narrow blade); lambnicker

Paring knife
This is a small knife with a thin, slightly flexible blade. It is used for all small hand-held work, such as shaping vegetables.

Cook's knives
The blades of these knives range in size from 10–30 cm (4–12 in). All cook's knives have a rigid blade and are used for a wide range of jobs including shredding, dicing and chopping. They are always used for trimming vegetables, meat, poultry or

game. The larger cook's knives can be used to chop through young porous bones of meat or poultry.

Filleting knives
The blades of these can range from 15–20 cm (6–8 in) or even longer. They have a very thin and flexible blade and are used to fillet fish.

Boning knives
The blade size of these ranges from 13–17 cm (5–6½ in). The blade can be straight or curved to suit large and small butchery. The blades are generally rigid but it is possible to buy boning knives with a slightly flexible blade. They are used to remove bones from joints of meat.

Steak knives
These range in size from 20–30 cm (8–12 in). A steak knife has a curved end and is specially designed to cut through raw meat. eg. sirloin and rump steaks.

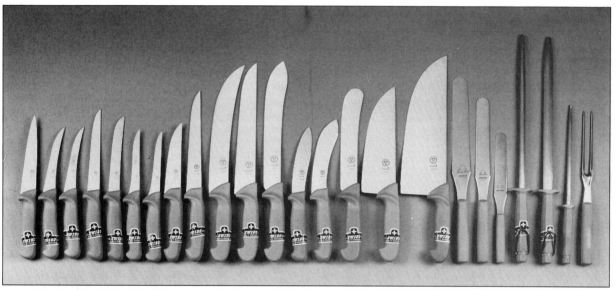

From left: boner (wide dagger blade); American boner (rigid blade); American boner (flexible); boner (rigid); Scandinavian boner; boner (flexible blade); boner (rigid); European boner; boner (long rigid blade); scimitar; European butcher's knife; Butcher's knife; sheep skinning knife; dough knife; Italian butcher's knife; heavy Italian butcher's knife; spatula; spatula; spatula; steel (round blade); steel (oval blade); household steel; fork

Slicers
These knives come in many different forms and are sometimes called by another name by manufacturers: you may see them called *meat knives* or *carvers*. The blades may have serrated or plain edges, and can be anything from 25–36 cm (10–14 in) long. Some have pointed ends while others have rounded ends. They are used to slice cooked meats, smoked salmon and even bread.

Deep-freeze knives
These knives are specially designed with a serrated blade to saw through frozen meat or fish. This type of knife is very specialised and is not part of every knife set.

Palette knives
These vary in length and width; some are plain edged while others have serrated edges. The blade is always flexible and rounded at the top. They are used for:
● moulding and shaping items, such as puréed potato
● turning items over whilst cooking, such as shallow-fried fish
● applying icing/cream to pastries and gateaux
● carving (serrated-edge palette knives only).

Oyster knife
This is a special knife used to prise open oyster shells. It has a rigid blade with a rounded point and a guard at the end of the handle.

Fork
A fork used by a chef has long and very sharp prongs. It is used to lift meat and poultry out of trays without piercing the flesh (which would allow the natural juices to escape).

Zesters
These are used to remove the thin layer of the outer skin from citrus fruits.

Vegetable peelers
These are used to peel all types of vegetables and some fruits. They have a sharp point at the end which is used to remove eyes and blemishes from vegetables.

Apple corers
These are used to remove the core from apples, pears, etc.

Poultry secateurs
These are used for cutting through poultry bones. Most have serrated blades and are spring loaded to make cutting easier.

Fish scissors
These are used to cut away fins and trim tails on all types of fish.

HOLDING A KNIFE

When practising your knife skills it is important to learn how to hold a knife in the correct manner.

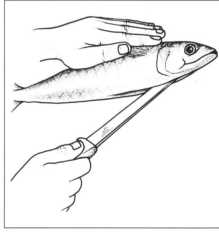

Left: the correct way to hold a boning knife
Right: the correct way to hold a filleting knife

If you were to hold a cook's knife in the same way that you hold a knife when eating you would have your hand around the handle and your first finger pointing down the blade. This is not the way to hold a cook's knife as it would not give you enough control. Instead, place the knife into your hand so that your thumb and first finger are grasping the blade but are not underneath the heel of the knife (or you will cut yourself). This may feel uncomfortable until you get used to it. When holding the knife correctly the blade should not be able to wobble about in your hand.

You would hold a filleting knife in the same way, but you should work with it keeping the blade horizontal (rather than vertical) in your hand most of the time.

The most notable exception to this method is the boning knife, which is generally held like a dagger. Note that the holding method depends on the joint being boned out.

Case study

One of your chefs has sustained a deep cut to their arm. The accident happened when they were walking past another chef who was boning a large joint of meat and the blade of the knife broke.
1 Why do you think the blade of the knife broke?
2 What do you think the reasons are for the person walking past to sustain the cut?
3 What action would you take to ensure that this does not occur again?

What have you learned

1 When carrying a knife around a busy kitchen, how should you hold it?
2 Why is it important to have only one knife on a choppng board at any one time?
3 Why should you always handle knives correctly?
4 Why do cooks need such a wide variety of knives to choose from?
5   What would you use the following knives for: filleting knife; cook's knife; steak knife?

Get ahead

1 Contact a knife supplier for further information, such as: Andrew Nisbet and Co Ltd, Unit 1, Waterloo Street, Old Market, Bristol 052 0PH.
2 Compare different sets of knives. Look at how they are made and compare their weights. Heavier knives often indicate quality.
3 If you are considering buying a knife, test several before making a choice. Is the handle, size and weight suited to you?
4 Watch other people using knives that you would not normally use. Notice the different holding techniques and methods used.

Receive, handle and store food deliveries

This chapter covers:
ELEMENT 1: **Receive and handle food deliveries**
ELEMENT 2: **Store food deliveries**

What you need to do

- Prepare receiving and storage areas ready for deliveries.
- Check the quality of delivered food items and their expiry date.
- Handle food items with care to minimise damage to food packaging.
- Ensure receiving areas are kept clean, tidy and free from rubbish and stores are secured from unauthorised access.
- Report any problems identified with food items promptly to the appropriate person.
- Work in an organised and efficient manner always prioritising your work according to organisational procedures and legal requirements.
- Store food items under the correct conditions according to food type.
- Rotate stock according to laid down procedures and following date order.
- Maintain accurate records for delivery goods and food items issued to individual departments.
- Ensure perishable food items are used or disposed of before their use-by-date.
- Report to the appropriate person food items at or below minimum stock levels.
- Maintain store areas under the correct conditions.

What you need to know

- Why it is important to keep delivery and storage areas free from rubbish and secure from unauthorised access.
- How to lift heavy and bulky items using safe techniques and methods.
- Why it is important to check food deliveries against expiry dates.
- How to identify the quality points of food items.
- Why and to whom you need to report any damaged deliveries identified.
- Why it is important to maintain a stock flow.
- How and why cooked and raw food items should be stored.
- When delivered, why frozen and chilled foods need to be stored immediately.
- Know what dangers from pest infestation are and how to recognise occurrences.
- Why stock control is important.

ELEMENT 1: Receive and handle food deliveries

Checking the delivered stores and handling them to minimise mechanical damage prior to storage is important. Equally important is to move deliveries carefully using safe methods and techniques to minimise the risk of injury or accidents to yourself or others you work with.

Large dry stores facility

PREPARATION FOR DELIVERIES

Food delivered can be divided into foods which are:
- stored in the kitchen for immediate use – bread, milk, vegetables and fresh fruit
- stored in the dry store
- stored in a fridge
- stored in a freezer.

You need to be prepared to check the:
- food order sheet with the delivery record
- that you can accommodate the delivered food items in the appropriate storage area
- date of each item to maintain stock rotation and use oldest stock first
- trolley or wheel trucks are available for use to move stores using safe methods and techniques
- food items to be returned, if any, are correct and that the delivery person removes these to the delivery van.

CHECKING FOOD DELIVERIES

The stores person receives a wide range of different types of food, fresh, dried, frozen, chilled and preserved foods requiring different storage conditions. When receiving stores you need to confirm certain basic requirements:

<table>
<tr><td>

Essential knowledge

</td><td>

You should check the following points.
- The order quantity, weight, size or volume tallies with the actual delivered food items
- Do the delivered items meet with quality indicators such as condition, temperature, appearance, freshness or specific quality indicators of each fresh food item, ie. fish meat, dairy etc.?
- The delivery note and paperwork tally with the order sheet and any discrepancies are notified to the driver, supplier and appropriate line manager.
- Confirm the paperwork by signing the necessary documentation.
- Confirm all packaging is intact and no mechanical damage has occurred during the delivery phase.
- Store each food item according to its specific storage requirements.

</td></tr>
</table>

Checking delivered food items for quality

Purchasing specifications can be drawn up by a business and provided for suppliers to use in attending to quality issues where food is concerned. The specifications

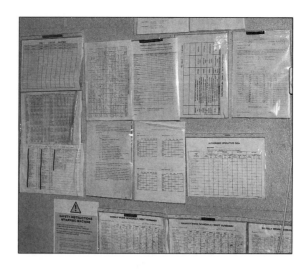

Daily delivery and order sheets

MEMORY JOGGER

Why is it important when receiving stores to check the weight, quantity and expiry date?

will set down the standards and descriptions of quality required for each food item. It might be first class fruits, A1 vegetables or prime cuts of meat. Where the delivered food does not match the specification and yet is charged at top rate prices the business can return the goods and insist they are replaced with quality foods according to the purchasing specifications.

Check food delivered by:

Smell – good food should smell fresh, not unpleasant but natural; any odd smell should invite closer inspection. Fish and dairy products need careful inspection where smell is concerned. If whole fish feels dry but not slimy, smell will confirm that it might not be fresh. Sometimes fishmongers might sell defrosted fish as fresh – can you tell the difference?

Taste – taste is one of the most essential quality indicators for good food, if in doubt about the taste of food check with someone more experienced who knows some of the problems that can and do occur with food. Food might taste rancid, acidic or tainted. Where this is found to be the case return the food to the supplier immediately: never delay with this type of problem.

Appearance – food when delivered should look fresh, clean, undamaged, visibly free from spoilage, slime, mould or fungal growth. One mouldy tomato or vegetable can and will 'turn' all the stock within days. Frozen foods need close inspection; excess ice on packaging might indicate partial thawing and re-freezing. Check for signs of freezer burn on foods.

Texture – does the food feel firm, soft, hard? How should it feel? What is the usual texture?

STOCK ROTATION AND STORAGE SYSTEMS

Storage of food in a safe and hygienic manner together with effective and efficient stock rotation is achieved by use of a simple system supported by modern equipment, ie. shelving, racking, bins etc.

Mobility of racking should be considered to make best use of the space available and for ease of cleaning. Inspection of all stored foods should be straightforward and should not involve large volumes of heavy food being moved by hand to check for infestation, contamination or general repair to walls and flooring.

Stock rotation is essential to ensure you use older foods first and newer purchases last. All foods are subject to rotation; check fresh and raw foods that are perishable daily, take a regular tally of foods to ensure stock is not being pilfered, stolen or lost.

Stock over-ordering which results in extended storage can lead to attack by rodents, insects, and mould growth developing in high humidity storage where ventilation is inadequate.

Remember: **First in First Out** – **Last in Last Out**

MEMORY JOGGER

Why do we use a stock rotation system?

Adopt a simple method of stock rotation, ensure new members of staff are aware of the system and make regular checks on stock levels. If food is stored incorrectly let your superior know; if food is damaged and being accepted, ensure that it is brought to someone's attention.

STORE AND STOCK RECORDS

- Keep stock records up-to-date.
- Always keep all delivery notes, order sheets and invoices in a safe place.
- Never rely on others; make certain that paper-work is managed correctly.
- Record information clearly and accurately. Use only metric units for all foods, as Europe does.
- Keep dry goods together in a logical order, with tally bin cards to assist in stock-taking.

Do this ✔
- Find out if purchasing specifications are provided for suppliers.
- What method of stock rotation is used in your store?
- Make a list of food items incorrectly stored. Why is this?
- Check a delivery of dry stores, make copies of the order and delivery sheets.
- How are dairy products stored? Check the temperature of the fridge units.

ACCEPT AND STORE MEAT AND POULTRY

Weighing meat items on delivery

Raw meat and poultry should be stored in separate fridges between −1 °C (30 °F) and +1 °C (34 °F), the relative humidity should be approximately 90%. Any humidity level above 95% will create microbial growth, with humidity levels below 85% causing evaporation and therefore weight loss. Stored raw meat and poultry should not touch the wall surface of the fridge or cool room.

Raw fresh meat joints should be hung on hooks in a cool room between −1 °C (30 °F) and +1 °C (34 °F). Drip trays should be placed under the meat to collect any blood. Cuts of meat should be wrapped in a lightly oiled greaseproof paper on a clean tray until required.

Delivered meat cuts should not be stored in the packaging they were delivered in. Small joints and whole cuts should be wiped with a damp cloth and wrapped as stated above.

Storing meat and meat products

Beef usually has a longer shelf life than lamb, pork or poultry. Processed raw meats such as sausages have the shortest shelf life and need careful stock rotation management to prevent contamination occurring.

Raw foods should always be kept separate from cooked foods during storage, unless only one fridge unit is available. If this is the case then all cooked foods should be trayed and stored at the top of the fridge and all raw meats at the bottom of the fridge to prevent juices from the raw meat contaminating the cooked meats. Raw meat at the base of the fridge would be cooked eventually.

Trayed, prepared meat storage

Safe storage times under hygienic conditions for raw meats at −1 ° (30 °F) are
- Beef   3 weeks
- Veal   1–3 weeks
- Lamb 1–2 weeks
- Pork   1–2 weeks
- Edible Offal 4 days

Meat of different types should not be stored together on the same tray. Drip trays and trays used for cuts of meat should be cleaned and replaced each day, otherwise blood juices will break down and contaminate the meat causing a bad odour and rancidity eventually causing the meat to be discarded. When preparing meat in the storage area to send to the kitchen, separate preparation tables and boards need to be used to prevent cross-contamination between raw and cooked meats. When fresh meat or poultry has been handled you must wash your hands both between different types of fresh meat and between handling raw or cooked meats. Consistency is sometimes difficult to maintain especially when you are busy, but you should never compromise on safety.

Raw meat should be kept refrigerated until required and not removed and left in a warm environment. If raw meat is cleaned with cold water it must be either dried thoroughly or used within 24 hours. Wet meat replaced into the fridge will break down very quickly, becoming sour and unfit for its purpose.

ACCEPT DELIVERY OF MEAT AND POULTRY

When meat and poultry are delivered always check for freshness, quality or bruising and see that meat is not sticky or has an unpleasant smell. Weigh each item to check that it corresponds with the delivery note and the order sheet. Remember to wipe clean the scales each time, washing your hands when handling different meats and poultry. Use paper on the scale pan to prevent contamination.

When best ends are delivered, check to see how much of the shoulder blade is left in. It should only be 1–2 cm at most; if you are unsure of the specifications then check with the chef or supervisor. Meat and poultry are very costly, the foods should be good quality, chilled when delivered, packaged separately and not thrown in one box or tray.

Check to see that mince is lean, not largely fat. Do not accept large percentages of fat such as butchers try to sell around topside joints, as you will find you are paying topside prices for fat.

MEMORY JOGGER

At which temperature should fresh meat be stored?

Do this

Meat is a complex but interesting subject. Make notes about:
● key quality points
● the correct storage method
● storage temperatures
● length of storage time.

Remember to 'hang' joints of meat, furred and feathered game. Tray cuts, small joints and minced items.

Case study

A delivery of meat is received and accepted for storage by the stores person. Upon checking you find the meat not to be of the quality required and when weighed it is found to be below the delivery note weights. When closely inspected by the chef the meat is sticky and has a slight smell.

1 What action should the stores person have taken upon receiving the meat?
2 Who should have been informed immediately the problems were discovered?
3 What action should the chef take in respect of the quality and quantity of the meat?
4 What possible explanation might be given for the meat being underweight?
5 What procedures would you change or apply to reduce the risk of this happening again?

ACCEPT AND STORE FISH

Fish at one time was a secondary food to that of meat and poultry, but over-fishing and increased consumption of fish as a daily food has pushed prices up. Fish is no longer the cheap alternative to meat or poultry, because we now pay a considerable price per kilo, so care when purchasing and storing of fish is not just essential but fundamental to effective food operations today.

At one time commercial fridges had a separate drawer for fish storage, where trays would hold the fish packed in ice until required. Today many smaller food operations do not have special fish storage units but use standard refrigeration. Because of the daily or regular availability of fish, both fresh and frozen, we purchase for daily requirements, or two to three times per week in most operations.

Fish needs to be fresh, firm, smell clean with no unpleasant odour, have a clean and bright appearance with a moist transparent outer slime, gills should be bright and the eyes not sunken.

If when delivered whole fish are not firm but soft, this can indicate it has just finished spawning and will not eat well, or that it is not fresh. When pressed with the fingers the impression should disappear. Stale fish tends to have a dry skin. Always check inside the belly flaps for signs of fresh blood, with the flesh attached to the bones.

When buying in fish fillets, are they fresh ? How do you know?

When buying in flat fish as fillets, have you equal numbers of white and dark skin fillets? Some fishmongers will give you 60–70% black fillets and the rest white, so check it out !

Fish can be purchased
● whole to be skinned, filleted and portioned
● skinned and filleted ready for portioning
● it can bought as steaks (darnes) or prepared to your requirements

- pre-frozen, pre-portioned ready to be finished
- frozen, portioned and finished ready to cook.

The fishmonger needs to know exactly how your fish should be prepared. Provide a detailed specification to remove any elements of poor communication. Fish farms, smokeries, specialist producers of shellfish and general fish sundries now enable us to purchase every type of fish from the whitebait to the shark steak. Many customers are today more adventurous and like to try different fish foods, including raw Japanese fish dishes – why not?

Points to remember about fish

- Fresh fish should be bought as near to time of use as possible.
- Ideally, it should be stored in ice in a fish refrigerator or at the base of a fridge operating at −1 °C to +1 °C (30–34 °F), covered, and the trays cleaned and changed daily.
- Frozen fish should be delivered and stored at −18 to −22 °C (0 to −8 °F).
- When accepting delivery of any fresh fish or shellfish food ensure the foods are fresh.
- Weigh all fish and shellfish products upon delivery.
- Check that live lobsters are alive, blue in colour and moving.
- How is the fish packed? Are the fish in separate boxes? Each fish should be boxed individually, to prevent cross-contamination of smell or juices.
- How many fillets were ordered, how many have been delivered?
- When accepting delivery of frozen fish is it frozen or thawing?
- Keep different deliveries separate; do not mix yesterday's delivery with today's.
- Only buy from a reputable trader; be careful of the back door purchase, cheap deal or someone doing you a favour!
- When in doubt, because of the cost of fish, always check if you are concerned about quality.
- All fresh fish or thawed frozen fish should be used within two days.
- Never re-freeze any fish that has been frozen.
- Keep smoked fish separate from fresh or frozen fish to avoid tainting other fish products. Smoked fish has a strong flavour which taints white fish especially.
- Shellfish that are alive, such as mussels and oysters, need to be tightly shut. Any that are open upon delivery should not be accepted.

Do this

- Which factors need to be checked when accepting a delivery of fresh meat?
- When should a delivery be signed for?
- Why is it important to store fresh raw meat and poultry when delivered?
- What action needs to be taken if fresh raw food is not fresh or does not meet with the purchasing specifications?
- Find out the unit costs for fresh meat and poultry from three different suppliers.
- Why is it required to weigh fresh or frozen fish upon delivery?
- Where and how should fresh fish be stored?

FRUIT AND VEGETABLES

Fruit and vegetables cover a vast range of individual products. To know all fruits and all vegetables is a difficult task given the ranges of exotic fruits, unusual vegetables and salad foods available for use today.

We have seen a great expansion of the variety of these once luxury food commodities and it is important to know exactly what you are ordering, how to know that it is fresh, ripe and competitively priced.

Knowing when fruit and vegetables are in season is a good guide to how much they should cost. Out-of-season foods cost much more because they have to be imported from other countries.

Specialist lettuce and unusual fruits carry a premium price out of season but still remain costly when in season. Chefs like to use these expensive foods, so check that your selling price reflects the increased food cost.

Accepting fruit deliveries

ACCEPT AND STORE VEGETABLES

The fresh vegetable market like that of fruit is one of the most difficult to purchase from. Vegetable produce is very perishable. If over-ripe produce is bought and not used quickly, the food deteriorates and becomes a loss. If purchased very under-ripe the eating quality is impaired affecting customer satisfaction.

Weather influences both availability and quality. When a vegetable item is in good supply then prices are low, when scarce prices are high. Some suppliers sometimes 'hike' prices artificially with certain vegetable foods. Imported vegetables will always cost more than home-grown produce.

A good sound knowledge of quality purchase points for fresh vegetables is essential where food quality can and is affected by so many variables: weather, supply, demand, storage, infestation from fly and blight etc.

When accepting fresh vegetables some key points should be used to identify the quality, degree of freshness and ripeness.

Root vegetables
Root vegetables such as carrot, beetroot, radish, celeriac, swede, salsify and parsnip need to be firm, clean, in season, free from bruising or decomposition, with no visible mould or fungal growth. Storage should be in bins or racks. Always remove the sack or bag to make the vegetables visible. Fine root shoots are an indication of age; when pressed, carrots should not be soft or spongy. As the season progresses the root vegetables are larger in size.

Small 'baby' vegetables are available at the start of the season. Baby vegetables today command high prices and are widely used for their artistic contribution to the modern chef's food palette.

MEMORY JOGGER

How are root vegetables best stored?

Open up any coloured netting which can disguise the true appearance of carrots and swede or parsnip. Root vegetables should be free from soil and undamaged by cuts from cultivation machinery. Stacking of root vegetables causes sweating and rot sets in, so keep them well ventilated.

Potatoes

These need to be fresh and firm with no signs of shoots growing, an indication of old age. There should not be any decomposition as this will quickly spread during storage. Open potato bags to view the produce you are buying. Storage needs to be in low humidity to prevent condensation.

Delivered in 25 kg brown paper sacks, potatoes should be kept in a cool dark store, away from strong sunlight which causes the potato to turn green, become hard and can be poisonous. Avoid stacking sacks of potato and keep stock rotation accurate by marking the delivery date on each sack.

Bulbs – leeks, onions, shallots and garlic

These should be stored in a low humidity to prevent condensation which can cause damage and spoilage. Care needs to be taken to check daily the conditions of bags of onions and shallots, removing any soft or decaying products to minimise spoilage of batch storage.

Leaves – cabbage, endive, spinach, watercress, lettuce, corn salad, kale, sprouts tops

These require cool storage with minimal handling to prevent mechanical damage to leaves. Green vegetables need to be stored on well ventilated racking, with salad leaves in a cool store kept in their delivery packaging. Green vegetables should be crisp, bright in colour and without signs of leaf decay or wilted appearance.

Flowers – broccoli, cauliflower, globe artichoke and calabrese

These should be stored in a cool place with a low humidity. Do not stack boxes or trays of flower vegetables, this causes damage and sweating resulting in decomposition. Avoid prolonged storage of these items, order in line with need.

Fruit vegetables

Courgette, marrow, aubergine, pepper, avocado pear, cucumber, gherkin and pumpkin require a storage temperature of 4–7 °C (39–45 °F). Store in a cool room or fridge on trays or in their delivery box but do not stack or crush the vegetables.

Seed and stem vegetables

Peas, beans, asparagus, celery and endive, peas and beans tend to be purchased frozen or fresh when in season. Storage or blanched stem and seed vegetables should be kept in cool dry conditions; some are damaged by condensation.

Fungi

Mushrooms, ceps, morels and chanterelles are best stored in their delivery container in a cool room. Many edible fungi are costly and need careful handling to prevent damage. Never stack units of mushrooms or special fungi.

Onions racked for storage

MEMORY JOGGER

Why should leaf vegetables be handled as little as possible?

From left to right: ceps, morels, button mushrooms, truffles

Store fungi at about 4–6 °C (39–43 °F), if stored in too cold a temperature freezing will damage this range of vegetables. Order in line with need; never over-order. To prevent wastage, excess fungi can be pickled or dried.

ACCEPT AND STORE EGGS

These may be hen, duck, goose, plover or quail eggs.

Widely used in all aspects of food preparation, the egg needs to be fresh, clean and undamaged. Without eggs the chef would be unable to complete dishes. It is essential that a minimum stock is kept to provide a continuous supply. Eggs are purchased by the case of 360 or half-case of 180, by the dozen or the half-dozen. Always purchase from a reputable dealer; eggs will take on the odour from strong smelling foods because of the porous shell. Store in a refrigerator at 1–4 °C (34–39 °F). Cracked eggs should be discarded and eggs other than hen eggs need to be checked carefully. Duck and goose eggs can harbour bacteria; only buy them from a supplier who is registered to sell such commodities.

Egg quality checklist

- The shell of the egg should be clean and undamaged.
- The egg white should be thick with a thin secondary white.
- The yolk needs to be firm, domed and round with a yellow/orangey colour.
- Eggs should smell pleasant with no strong or bad odour (hydrogen sulphide).

As eggs age the white becomes watery – evident when eggs are fried as the fat will spit due to the volatility of the water and oil mixture. Fresh eggs are compact where the primary and secondary white supports the yolk. Eggs are a risk food and need careful handling and storage to prevent the spread of harmful bacteria such as *salmonella enteriditis*. Eggs are used to thicken, enrich, colour, bind, clarify, garnish and aerate dishes.

Check that eggs meet the quality points listed

Size grade and weight of eggs	
GRADE 1	70 g
GRADE 2	65 g
GRADE 3	60 g
GRADE 4	55 g
GRADE 5	50 g
GRADE 6	45 g
GRADE 7	under 45 g

Eggs can be purchased as dried egg white, frozen pasteurised egg and spray-dried egg. Used more in the bakery and confectionery trades, albumen substitutes are used for meringue and royal icing.

Do this

- What is the reason for checking fresh fruit and vegetables daily?
- Why are foods more expensive out of season?
- List four ways in which vegetables are preserved.
- Where are eggs best stored? How can freshness be identified?
- What is the reason for caution when using duck or goose eggs?
- How can food stores be made safe from unauthorised access ?

ACCEPT AND STORE BREAD ITEMS

Accepting bread deliveries

Traditionally bread was purchased sliced or unsliced or as whole items such as French sticks and roll products, purchased daily. Today bread items are available par-baked, frozen ready-to-bake and as gas-packed bake-off products. Gas-packed bread is placed in the bag and backwashed with an inert gas to preserve the par-baked bread product until opened and baked to add colour. Fresh bread should be stored in a well ventilated room; bread needs to be arranged to allow accurate stock rotation to occur.

Ambient storage is adequate providing the packaging is not damaged. Frozen bread food items that are ready-to-bake should be stored at −18 °C (0 °F) and be used according to the manufacturer's directions. Freshly purchased bread items will last for up to four days if stored in the correct conditions. Always check the use-by date. Stale bread can be dried and used for breadcrumbs or rusk, bread pudding, soaked to add bulk for stuffings, or diced up into croutons as a garnish.

Rolls need to be used within 24 hours or frozen after 12 hours and used within one month of freezing to maintain some freshness, although de-frosted bread items tend to be dry unless served hot. Bread does not go dry, but the sugar content of the baked bread crystallises; when stale bread is toasted it becomes moist again because the crystals are dissolved – melted by the heat.

Always check the date of the bread delivered, check that packaging is not damaged and no mould is evident on sliced bread. Many delivery persons smoke and handle bread products without washing their hands. Check to see that the suppliers have staff who are both qualified to at least basic food hygiene standards and insist on a code of health and safety in the handling of bread food items.

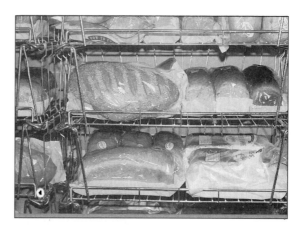

Bread wrapped and racked for storage

ACCEPT AND STORE CAKES AND BISCUITS

Cakes and biscuits wrapped and racked for storage

A dry store should have a relative humidity of R.H. 60–65% , be cool, well lit and ventilated with adequate storage space to enable effective stock rotation. Generally cakes that are moist products ie. finished or filled with buttercream, sugar-based filling, fudge icing etc. need to kept cool. Fresh cream products need to be refrigerated below 5 °C (41 °F) to prevent contamination and spoilage.

Dry cake and biscuit products such as sponges, sweet and savoury biscuits should be stored in dry storage at a temperature of 5–10 °C (41–50 °F) . Frozen cakes need to be defrosted in the fridge and not in ambient conditions. Cake mixtures that are powder based (convenience) should be stored at least 45 cm off the floor in the dry food storage area. Storing cakes and biscuit is made simple by following the storage instructions on the packaging for each individual food item. Never over-order in this area as many cake and biscuit commodities have a relatively short shelf-life; use in strict stock rotation and keep a log of the use-by dates for each cake or biscuit range.

ACCEPT AND STORE DAIRY FOODS

Accepting a delivery of dairy products

MEMORY JOGGER

Below which temperature should dairy items be stored?

The acceptance and storage of this range of food commodities requires sound knowledge and efficient skills to manage the safe storage and economic use of these food items. Foods such as milk, cream (ideal foods for bacterial growth), butter, cheese, eggs should be placed in the refrigerator below 5 °C (41 °F). The quality of cheese is affected by prolonged storage as cheese will develop a soft stodgy texture. As soon as dairy foods are delivered they should be refrigerated. All cheese needs to be wrapped or contained to prevent them from being tainted by other foods.

Imitation cream should also be refrigerated when delivered. Never store crates of milk below fresh meat which might drip juices on to the milk resulting in contamination. When delivered, dairy food items should be checked for damage to cartons, bottle-top damage by birds and leaks or penetration of packaging due to poor storage during transportation.

The rotation of dairy food commodities is essential to ensure that dairy products are fresh at the time of preparation and production. Always check the use-by date. Dairy foods part-used and returned to the fridge need to be sealed or covered to prevent contamination.

Chilled storage of dairy products

ACCEPT AND STORE DRY GOODS

Dry goods in storage. Notice that heavier, canned products are stored below the softer packaged products.

Dry goods include sugars, pulses, cereals, flour, spices and herbs, jams and pickles, condiments, bottles or jars, canned and tinned foods, bread, cakes and biscuits. Areas used for the storage of dry food commodities need to be cool, well ventilated and lit with a relative humidity of R.H. 60–65%.

Sufficient space is required to store single or multi-pack dry food items which allows effective stock rotation to occur. Internal walls should be free from cavities; wall surfaces should be impervious.

Dry goods as the name implies covers all those foods of a dry nature but includes foods that are tinned or packaged and any non-perishable commodity. Dry goods need to be stored off the floor or in storage bins which can be sealed.

Tinned goods need to be stored in cases or as individual units depending on the unit of issue or use. When delivered, check to see they are not bulging or damaged; look for leaks or staining to the box. Use in strict rotation: first in first out – last in last out.

Dry storage needs to be fly and vermin proof, adequately shelved with bins for storage of bulk items. The effective storage of dry goods revolves around the method of stock rotation used.

Be sure you know the volume of dry stores needed to maintain a continuous supply to the various catering operations. Store each dry food commodity in the best ideal conditions given the availability and design of the storage space. Some catering operations have purpose-built rooms, many only a cupboard or small room.

Essentially, keep the dry store clean, tidy and well ventilated. Keep strong-smelling foods separate from more mellow foods and never store cleaning materials with dry food products.

Dry goods storage

Do this

- How can stale bread be utilised?
- Check to see if cleaning material is stored in the same room as food items.
- What signs might indicate infestation in dry stores and store rooms?
- What conditions should cakes and biscuits be stored in?
- Why is it important to keep receiving areas clean, tidy and free from rubbish?
- What is the reason for keeping a minimum stock level?

CLEANLINESS

Cleaning is the systematic application of energy to a surface, substance or equipment with the aim of removing or preventing dirt.

All food storage areas not only need to be cleaned but must be kept clean on a consistent and regular basis. In many establishments the cleanliness of the kitchens and food storage areas has been found to be, to say the least, inadequate and at best, unacceptable. The implementation of more rigorous inspection by officials has eradicated some of the more unprofessional food operators although many staff would still benefit from training in hygiene management at basic, intermediate and advanced levels.

You must take responsibility to *improve standards of cleanliness* where the preparation and sale of food to any person is concerned. Stores need to be cleaned daily and weekly with a monthly deep clean to ensure safe and hygienic storage of food items.

The packaging, shelving, storage bins, fridges and freezers need to be cleaned weekly to prevent the build-up of ice or contamination from raw food juices and debris. Shelves need to be cleaned regularly; often dust and debris are unseen if bottles, jars and containers are never removed to clean.

Keep *waste bins* and *refuse areas* hygienically clean. Daily management will keep a check on infestation, contamination and general dirt.

Consistently ensure that staff who touch their heads in any way always wash their hands. We all have habits and these need to be addressed to improve the qualitative handling of food from arrival in store to delivery to the dish.

Cleaning can be a complicated subject involving specialist materials, equipment and processes but there is no excuse for unclean storage or food preparation areas. Food packaging, boxes and containers need careful and considered management, these elements are the responsibility of all who work, supervise or manage within the food industry.

FOOD PACKAGING

Packaging includes cans, bottles or jars, packets or boxes, bags or sacks.

Packaging serves the purpose of assisting in the preservation of food. It protects against water vapour, light, dust, oxygen, dirt, weight loss, mechanical damage and infestation by insects and micro-organisms. Packaging materials if not sterile could introduce the minimum of contamination ie. pathogens.

Packaging covers
● Tins
● Jars
● Bottles
● Cans
● Boxes
● Sacks
● Bags

Packaging can be
● Plastic – rigid/flexible
● Glass
● Cardboard
● Paper
● Foil
● Tin

The Department of Health produces leaflets outlining temperature controls for food delivery.

Cans

We use a large variety of canned foods including fruit, tomato purée, vegetables and concentrates, condensed milk, jam, curd, marmalade, fruit juices, baked beans, cooked meats, pâté, soups, sauces and stocks. Canned food can contain salt or sugared liquid solutions which preserve the food item by osmosis. The risk of contamination from canned food today is low. Reactions can occur inside canned food which cause a build up of gas which causes the top of the can to bulge; such a can needs to be discarded. Always check before accepting canned foods that the cans are sound, undamaged and not bulging. Look for signs of age; the boxes containing the canned food should be clean, unbroken and coded. Storing canned goods in high or humid temperatures can induce damage by internal corrosion of the tin seal, rusting in extreme cases and eventually pin-holing, all leading to contaminated food unfit for human consumption.

High acid foods such as fruit if stored longer than is advised by the manufacturer are subject to bulging or blowing. Tins of ham, tongue or other processed meats should be stored in a dry good store and chilled prior to use for ease of slicing. Opened canned products should be placed in a suitable covered container, preferably stainless steel, glass or plastic but not aluminium and kept refrigerated. When opened always inspect the content of the can, smell, taste and confirm that the food is fresh, untainted by metal or fermentation.

Canned food can be stored for up to 5 years depending on the type of food. Always follow the recommended storage time of the manufacturer.

Bottles or jars

Food delivered and accepted in jars or bottles includes milk, fruit, jams, pickles and dressings. The bottle should not be cracked or chipped but sound and sealed. Check to see if the lid seal has been broken or damaged: these should be rejected upon delivery. Store them where damage is unlikely to occur and away from strong sunlight which can cause a 'greenhouse effect' to trigger the production of gases, fermentation and spoilage. Keep opened bottles and jars in the fridge. Never wash out and use milk bottles to store food in, or any jars that are not sterile.

Left: bottle and jar storage. Right: packet storage

Packets or boxes

Food delivered in packets or boxes should be undamaged and tally with the order sheet and delivery note. Always check for signs of ageing as torn or crushed packaging might indicate damage to the seal of dried foods and possible contamination.

Rotate stock and check the use-by date suggested by the manufacturer. Look for signs of leaking packets where contents have spilled into the delivery carton.

Some deliveries are badly handled or crushed by over-stacking, be aware of infestation from cockroaches, silverfish or other insects and check for vermin damage. Never accept a delivery just because the driver says the consignment is all there. Count the goods in and check each carton, package or box with the driver, it's no good complaining weeks later when problems are discovered.

Cereals and dry goods should be sealed, any split or ripped packaging should be identified and a credit note issued by the supplier to compensate for such problems.

Purchase dry goods from a range of traders, use only recognised companies you know to have customer care and customer satisfaction as their priority and never accept second best. If you pay the price ensure the goods are of merchantable quality and fit for their advertised use.

Bags or sacks

Bulk foods are delivered in bags or sacks eg. flour, cereals, pulses, dry pre-mixes, specialist additives. Always store sacks or bags of food on pallets off the floor surface. Use effective stock rotation methods and, with a pen, mark the delivery date on them. Check that you know which bag of flour is which – many do not say whether they are plain, strong or self-raising.

Check for signs of vermin attack, nibbled or gnawed edges, damaged or cut sacks as these should not be accepted. Bags should be sealed and if open must be rejected: once accepted you have taken responsibility for the health and safety of that food commodity.

Damp or stained bags or sacks need to be rejected. If infestation is found, seal the unit in a secure plastic bag or liner, remove the food from other food stores and inform the suppliers. If you cannot get satisfaction then call your Environmental Health Officer – this always ensures the suppliers conform to their responsibilities.

> **MEMORY JOGGER**
>
> Why should storage areas be vermin proof?

Stacked potatoes

Do this

- What cleaning schedule is used in your store areas?
- Why is care needed to check packaging on delivery?
- Find out how VAT and credit notes are dealt with by the store person.
- What measures can be taken to prevent infestation in a food store?

MANUAL HANDLING

Safety when moving stores

Lifting bulky or awkward shaped items such as bags of potatoes can lead to back injury which accounts for a large percentage of injuries suffered in industry. When moving these types of packages you should know how to lift and move them in a safe manner.

Where lifting and moving equipment such as trolleys and wheel trucks are provided or available, then use these pieces of equipment to minimise the risk of personal injury. Never over-stack boxes or packages as this might damage the goods or, more seriously, be the cause of an accident.

Essential knowledge

- Where possible ask for help to move bulky or awkward items.
- Having moved a large quantity of food stores, rest before moving subsequent stores, allowing sufficient time to regain your strength.
- Never attempt to move stores if you feel ill or unwell.
- If the stores need to be moved some distance do this in stages, not all at once.
- Check that the route is clear of obstacles and obstructions.
- Check the floor is not damp, wet or soiled to minimise the risk of accidents.
- Read up on the *Manual Handling Operations Regulations 1992*.

What have you learned?

1 Why should store areas be secured from unauthorised access at all times?
2 Why must deliveries tally with both the order and delivery documentation?
3 What action should you take if delivered items are damaged or missing when receiving store deliveries?
4 Why should storage areas be kept clean and free from rubbish?
5 Why do we store frozen and chilled foods immediately?
6 Why is it necessary to report problems with delivered food items immediately to the appropriate person?

ELEMENT 2:   Store food deliveries

TYPES OF STORAGE CONDITIONS

Lighting

Lighting of food storage and food areas in general tends to be overlooked which in some cases leads to eye strain. Fluorescent lighting strips need to be protected in case of breakage and should be fitted with diffusers. Store rooms without natural light need adequate illumination to ensure floor spaces behind and under shelving can be seen easily for cleaning and checking for infestation.

Kitchen areas are preferable where natural light and internal lighting are balanced to ensure comfortable vision during prolonged periods in kitchens where reflective glare can cause tiredness and fatigue. Corridors, walkways and secondary rooms need to be well lit to maintain a safe and secure working environment. Defects and problems with lighting should always be reported immediately.

Walk-in fridges and cold rooms should illuminate on opening the door to prevent accidents occurring. Basement or semi basement kitchens and stores need particular types of lighting and it is essential to seek the advice of a specialist to advise on the correct type and strength of lighting to ensure safe working conditions prevail. Fittings need to be placed with care to ensure effective illumination and ease of cleaning. When placed over stoves or moist cooking areas such as bain-marie, water-tight diffuser covers need to be used.

MEMORY
JOGGER

Why does a food
store need to be
adequately
ventilated?

Ventilation

Good ventilation of stores and kitchen areas is essential to keep the relative humidity (R.H.) in balance for the types of foods being stored and the kitchen area free from the build-up of heat, steam which causes condensation, grease and the ideal conditions for contamination. Working conditions can be seriously undermined where inadequate ventilation occurs. Foods are greatly affected by ventilation and expert advice should be sought when deciding on the type and position of a new ventilation system.

Natural ventilation often needs to be supported by mechanical venting systems to create a balanced flow of clean air in and poor air out – usually 85% input capacity to rated output capacity. Equipment producing steam and moisture needs to be covered with canopies and have direct extraction via ducting.

Ducting

Ducting filters need to be cleaned and filters replaced regularly. This prevents a build-up of grease and dust which is a fire hazard well known in food preparation and production areas. Poor ventilation not only reduces the shelf-life of many dry stored foods but can also damage your health. Extractors need to extract to an outside wall but should not be so placed that they pollute the air with food odour and dust eg. below the restaurant windows or guest accommodation.

Do this

- Find out what type of lighting is fitted to your own food storage area.
- Check to see where tinned meats are stored.
- How many types of dried preserved food can you find in your food store?
- Draw a plan of the ventilation systems to keep ambient and humid atmospheres balanced.

Essential knowledge

- Dry food stores shelving should be at least 45 cm off the floor.
- Food should not be stored in contact with the floor.
- Dry stores should be airy and well ventilated.
- Dry stores must be fly and vermin proof.
- Adequate shelving is needed.
- Dry stores must be cool and dry.
- The stores must be secured by lock, key or cage.

STORAGE OF DIFFERENT FOOD TYPES

Ambient food storage

Where dry or non-perishable foods are to be stored at an ambient temperature, in relation to the environment this means the normal or customary conditions of temperature and humidity. Each storage area might have a varying ambient temperature and humidity level, but one with approximately 50–60% relative humidity is suitable as ambient storage. Coastal areas will have problems with ambient storage where the air humidity is high, being at sea level, and this needs to be considered when planning or siting a store area.

Dry herbs and spices can loose their qualities of flavour and aroma if stored in too dry an atmosphere, whereas biscuit and cereal products will retain their dry texture well.

Storing food at ambient temperatures can allow the development of harmful bacteria if the foods are high risk, high protein based food items and if left uncovered for an extended period of time before being chilled, refrigerated or frozen.

Chilled foods and storage

Chilling refers to the temperature of cooling or storage temperature used to preserve foods and food items for a short period of up to five days. Food is chilled down to 3 °C (38 °F) using blast chiller machines which chill food down to a chill temperature for storage.

Never re-chill or re-freeze food that has already been chilled or frozen unless it has been safely cooked from its raw, chilled or frozen state. Cold chilling of foods and chilled storage only *delays* or *retards* the decay and decomposition of food, but does not prevent it entirely.

The purpose of chilling is to slow down the rate at which food is spoilt. Chilling covers a temperature range from ambient temperature down to near freezing point but not actually frozen. Chilling operates at temperatures of 1–5 °C (34–41 °F) .

Wrapped, packed and trayed meat in chilled storage

Cook-chill food production

This is a system of conventional production methods but foods are chilled rapidly within 90 minutes and stored at 3 °C (37 °F) for up to 5 days.

Chill cabinets and units should be checked regularly, temperature recordings should be taken twice daily and a log kept. A thermometer and probe should be used in conjunction with sterile wipes to prevent cross-contamination occurring. Chilled foods should only be held for the minimum time and used as soon after preparation as is possible. High protein, dairy and high risk products need to be managed carefully so as not to build up too large a stock of chilled commodities. There can be a tendency to mix foods in chilled storage which should be avoided.

Frozen foods

Frozen foods are now a mainstay in preservation processes for society both from a domestic viewpoint and a commercial one. We all use daily frozen food items for breakfast, lunch, dinner, snack or special occasion. Large industrial caterers and the three-bedroom guest house manage a freezer unit to store and use frozen food items which cover every conceivable food type.

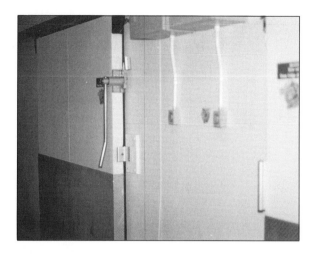

A modern 'walk-in' freezer storage unit

It is important that the trainee chef, storekeeper, manager, proprietor – or any person involved in the food chain where frozen food is used, stored or transported – should work effectively to reduce waste, rotate stock correctly, and wrap products to be frozen safely in order to ensure the food is safe to eat when cooked, reheated or served cold.

The management of frozen food is an area where losses are incurred through not keeping accurate ledgers of freezer contents, where food at the base or back of freezers is ignored until freezer-burnt and then has to be discarded.

What types of food are frozen?

Almost all food can be frozen and stored for up to three months depending on the type of food and freezer unit being used. Fruit pulps to fancy fish, pastry to pies, gateaux and torten, icecream and mousses, meat, poultry, cuts, joints and finished *à la carte* ready meals all find a place in the modern domestic and commercial freezer unit: frozen sauces, bread products, smoked and speciality goods, the list is endless.

Freezing food will not improve the quality of any food. Large ice crystals that form while slow freezing occurs, expand to denature the connective structure of foods and alter the texture and finish when thawed for use; the frozen strawberry is a classic example.

Storage times and temperatures for freezers

*	not above −6 °C (21 °F) (7 days).
**	not above −12 °C (10 °F) (one month).
***	not above −18 °C (0 °F) (three months).
****	not above −18 °C to −25 °C (0 °F to −13 °F) (three months plus).

MEMORY JOGGER

How long can food marked with three stars *** be stored for?

All frozen foods should be used within the time specified by the manufacturer. Salad vegetables, single cream, eggs, bananas and non-homogenised milk should not be frozen. The packaging of foods will affect the freezing of both the food itself and those foods stored near packaged products. Boxes of sheet puff pastry can act as an insulator which can prevent foods trapped underneath from freezing so careful attention must be paid to the method of stacking and packaging food items to be frozen.

Ice build-up on packaging when frozen food is delivered can mean that fluctuation in freezing temperatures has occurred and these items need to be rejected.

Quality frozen packed foods will have a light frost but not icy build-up of frozen water/moisture on the packaging. Be careful and vigilant that all icecream products are frozen hard on delivery. Icecream products must be stored in a separate freezer unit.

Thawing of frozen food

Defrosting of frozen food can and does lead to food poisoning due to a lack of knowledge, incompetent management and inadequate storage equipment. Thin, small or pre-portioned food items can be cooked from their frozen state. Small frozen food items should be defrosted in the fridge. Large joints of meat, game or poultry need to be hygienically defrosted before being cooked. Read the manufacturer's instruction for defrosting the frozen food item, stick rigidly or as near as is possible to the conditions for defrosting as recommended.

Frozen poultry and turkeys or meat joints that are cooked where the centre is still frozen are likely to cause food poisoning as the cooking process will melt the icy centre while cooking the outside and thus encourage the growth of harmful bacteria. Thawing of turkeys in particular needs to be managed professionally. The bird must be removed in good time from the freezer to allow for natural thawing to occur. A 9 kg oven ready turkey can take 30 hours at ambient room temperature (10 °C/50 °F) to defrost.

Essential knowledge	Frozen poultry present the most risk if not defrosted correctly, it is important to:
	● Thaw in a cool room completely at a temperature of between 10–15 °C (50–59 °F) but not exceeding 15 °C (59 °F).
	● Ensure the flesh is pliable and there is no ice remaining in the body cavity. Cool clean running water can be used as a method of thawing, rather than a warm kitchen environment.
	● Always cook within 24 hours of being thawed.
	● Cook thoroughly until the juices of the leg run clear.
	● Refrigerate within 90 minutes of cooking/cooling whichever is the sooner.
	● Always wash your hands after handling frozen produce, especially between uncooked and cooked foods.
	● Plastic wrapping around frozen poultry, ducks, guinea fowl must be removed from the frozen bird.

Food freezer temperatures

Icecream	−22 °C to −18 °C (−8 °F to 0 °F)
Meat and Fish	−20 °C to −16 °C (−4 °F to +4 °F)
Frozen Foods	−20 °C to −16 °C (−4 °F to +4 °F)

Never place warm or hot foods into freezer units. Rotate freezer stock and check for signs of freezer burn where products take on a dry white appearance.

Do this	● Check the freezers for food suffering from the effects of freezer burn.
	● Find out what method of defrosting frozen foods is used in your stores.
	● See if cooked and raw foods are stored together. Are they stored correctly?
	● Is the store equipped with two sinks for food handling, and if not why not?
	● How does the store person log food in the chest freezer?

STORE COOKED FOOD

Cooked foods should be kept in separate refrigeration or storage and away from uncooked food. If raw and cooked foods need to be in the same fridge then raw foods should always be placed on the bottom with cooked foods at the top.

This prevents juices from raw meats contaminating cooked foods which are not subject to subsequent cooking. Cooked food items need to be cooled quickly and stored in a refrigerator immediately when cool. Cooked pies, pasties and sausage rolls require storage in a fridge at 7 °C (45 °F) with good air movement to keep the pastry dry and crisp.

Invariably, pastry becomes waxy and damp through storage in cold or high humidity conditions. Stock rotation is important to prevent stale foods being used because of poor stock control system. Pies, such as game or pork where gelatine has been added after baking should be stored below 5 °C (41 °F).

Case study

A selection of quiches are prepared and produced for a hospitality buffet. At the conclusion of the event feedback from waiting staff suggested a number of complaints regarding soggy pastry.
1   What reasons can be given for this type of problem?
2   How can you prevent this problem occurring again?
3   What checks can be suggested to ensure quality presentation of high risk foods such as quiches and dairy products in general?

COOKED FOOD PRODUCTS

Temperature

It is now the responsibility of each catering employer and employee to ensure storage is maintained either below 8 °C (46 °F) or above 63 °C (145 °F) for all cooked foods which are liable to the growth of bacteria and the production of toxins.

New regulations released in 1995 replace previous regulations relating to the storage temperature of food items. The new act is called *The Food Safety (Temperature Control) Regulations 1995.*

UNCOOKED FOODS

Uncooked food needs to be ordered, checked on delivery and stored according to its food type, as described previously. Never store uncooked and cooked food together if it can be avoided. If you must store uncooked food with cooked food store the uncooked below the cooked food in a fridge or cold room. Keep uncooked foods away from the walls of cold storage rooms, fridges and chill boxes. Order in line with need, over-ordering is a problem in the management cycle of hygienic and professional care of food.

Do this

- Find out how old the fridges and freezers are in your kitchen.
- Are twice daily readings taken of all fridges and freezers?
- Check where fridges and freezers are sited. Why is this important?
- Why are meat joints hung? Look to see if fresh meat is stored correctly.

PRESERVED FOODS

Preserved foods date back to mankind's beginnings when food was salted or dried – long before the invention of the fridge.

Preserved foods cover a wide range of food types; those dealt with here are the major foods more commonly purchased for food storage and subsequent use.

Food preservation is the treatment of food to delay or prevent and inhibit spoilage and the growth of pathogenic organisms which would result in the food being unfit for human consumption.

Types of food preservation

- low or high temperature
- dehydration – moisture control
- chemicals
- restriction of oxygen – controlled atmosphere
- smoking
- irradiation

Low temperature preservation

This slows down the speed of enzymic reaction. It covers a range of low temperature processes such as air-blast freezing, cryogenic, plate freezing, fluidized-bed freezing and the pellofreeze system. It can be carried out:
- above freezing (in a refrigerator)
- at freezing (in a chiller as for chilled meat)
- below freezing (in a freezer)

High temperature preservation

This includes:
- pasteurisation
- sterilisation
- Ultra Heat Treatment (UHT)
- cooking

Dehydration

Drying of food involves reducing the moisture content below 25%. It can be done by:
- sun drying
- artificial drying using drums, hot air, tunnel or spray roller
- accelerated freeze-drying

Many convenience foods are preserved by drying; water is added to reconstitute the food item. All dried preserved foods need to be stored in a low relative humidity and kept dry, stored off the floor on racking or shelving. Check any packages that have been damaged during transit or storage, look for mould growth on dry preserved foods kept for long periods of time. Always consult the manufacturer's suggested best-before date.

Chemical methods of preservation

The most common chemical methods of food preservation involve sugaring, salting or curing processes. There are also several acid preservation methods.
- salt (curing)
- nitrates and nitrites
- sugar
- benzoic acid / sodium benzoate
- sorbic acid / potassium sorbate
- sulphur dioxide / sodium sulphite
- acetic acid / lactic acid
- sodium propianate / calcium propionate
- antibiotics

Controlled atmosphere

This method is becoming more widely used and many bread, salad and vegetable products are preserved using the MAP method which means modified atmosphere packaging. Gas replaces most of the oxygen around the product to slow down spoilage. These products still need to be preserved by using temperature control ie. chillers and refrigeration.

Smoking

Food is pickled or brined and suspended over smouldering hardwood chips such as ash or oak wood. The foods become partially dehydrated and acquire a particular flavour and colour. Preserved smoked products must still be refrigerated below 3 °C (37 °F) to prevent the development of toxins.

Food irradiation

Food is subjected to ionising radiation from gamma rays emitted via an isotope (cobalt 60). Insects, parasites and most forms of microbes are destroyed whereas spores and toxins can remain. *The Food (Control of Irradiation) Regulations, (1990)* authorised the irradiation of food in the United Kingdom. Irradiation of food is subject to very strict licensing controls and all irradiated food must be labelled in accordance with *The Food Labelling (Amendment) (Irradiated Food) Regulations, (1990)*. Foods irradiated more commonly include fish, chicken, potatoes, onions, spices and strawberries.

What have you learned

1 Why is it important to keep food storage areas well lit, well ventilated and at the correct temperature?
2 Why is it important to store cooked and raw foods separately?
3 Why when receiving chilled and frozen foods is it important to store them immediately?
4 What are the dangers of pest infestation?
5 Why should a constant flow of stock be maintained?
6 Why is stock control important?

Get ahead

1 Investigate computerised stock control systems. On what basis do they track stock movements and what data is needed to set up the system prior to going live?
2 Look at your store documentation. Are there any areas not covered by the paperwork, for instance delivery temperature monitoring log record sheet?
3 Does your organisation have purchasing specification details, if so which goods do they cover and why?
4 Determine the approximate value of stocks held for your store area and suggest ways in which this might be minimised.

Clean and maintain cutting equipment

This chapter covers:
ELEMENT 1: **Clean cutting equipment**
ELEMENT 2: **Maintain cutting equipment**

What you need to do
- Clean cutting equipment in accordance with laid down procedures using the correct cleaning equipment and materials.
- Dismantle and reassemble cutting equipment correctly.

- Plan your time efficiently and appropriately in order to meet daily schedules.
- Handle, use and store cleaning agents and materials correctly

What you need to know
- The reasons for cleaning cutting equipment.
- How to handle and use cleaning agents.
- The main contamination threats when cleaning.

- How to handle, clean and store cutting equipment correctly.
- How to deal with unexpected situations.

ELEMENT 1: **Clean cutting equipment**

WHAT IS *CLEANING*?

Cleaning is the removal of all food residues and any dirt or grease that may have become attached to work surfaces. equipment and utensils during the preparation and cooking of food

To clean effectively, we need to use *energy*. This can be in the form of:
1 *physical energy*. For example: scrubbing by hand or mechanical equipment. This removes any food debris which may have remained on cooking equipment or utensils.
2 *heat energy (thermal)*. For example: hot water or steam. This helps to melt grease and fat, making it easier to scrub clean. Heat energy can also be used to destroy bacteria. This will only happen when the temperature is above 82 °C (180 °F).
3 *chemical energy*. For example: the use of detergents and disinfectants. Note the following:
   - a *detergent* will dissolve grease and fat but will not kill bacteria
   - a *disinfectant* removes infection (reduces bacteria to a safe level) but will not dissolve fats
   - a *steriliser* will kill all living micro-organisms
   - a special cleaning product called a *sanitiser* combines the effects of both detergent and disinfectant.

> **MEMORY JOGGER**
>
> At what temperature does water destroy bacteria?

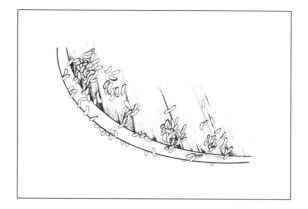

A knife blade that looks clean may harbour bacteria visible only under a microscope

THE REASONS FOR CLEANING

All food handlers, like doctors, have a *legal and a moral responsibility* to their customers. It is up to you to prevent outbreaks of food poisoning. The reasons we clean are:
● to comply with the law
● to remove any food debris on which bacteria may grow. This will reduce the risk of food poisoning
● to enable disinfectants to be effective on work and equipment surfaces
● to remove any food which may attract food pests, eg. insects, rodents, birds and domestic pets
● to reduce the contamination of food by foreign matter, eg. dust, flaking paint, grease from mechanical equipment
● to make the area in which you are working a pleasant and safe place
● to make a favourable impression on customers.

PLANNING YOUR TIME

In order to be effective and efficient you need to consider the best method of working, so that cleaning is carried out in a methodical and systematic way.
1 Identify the areas, equipment or utensils that you will be required to clean and when they need to be ready to use again.
2 Plan ahead: have all your cleaning equipment and materials ready.
3 *Clean as you go* is the basic motto, but always check the most appropriate time to clean:
    ● mincing machines
    ● slicing machines
    ● rotary knife (vegetable) chopping machines.

HEALTH, SAFETY AND HYGIENE

Make sure that you are familiar with the general points given in Unit NG1 (pages 2–33).

Mechanical cutting equipment is extremely dangerous: every year there are thousands of accidents, some resulting in serious injury and amputation of limbs. The dangers associated with cutting equipment should never be underestimated.

Always ensure that you have been fully trained before cleaning or dismantling any cutting equipment.

Persons under 18 are forbidden by law to clean cutting equipment.

> **MEMORY JOGGER**
>
> What is the minimum age you must be to clean cutting equipment?

THE PRESCRIBED DANGEROUS MACHINES ORDER 1964

This specifies that it is illegal for anyone to operate or clean certain machines unless they have been properly instructed or trained. The following machines fall within this category'.

● mincing machines (worm type)
● chopping machines (rotary knife bowl type)
● mixing machines (with attachments for mincing, slicing, shredding, etc.)
● slicing machines (with circular knife)
● potato chipping machines
● food processors.

All the above mentioned machinery must have clear warning signs stating the danger of the equipment.

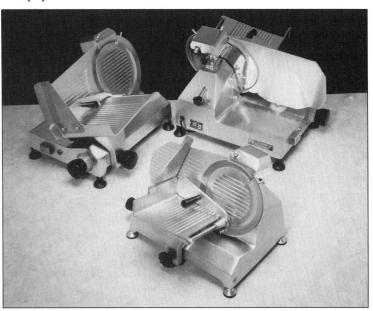

Always ensure that you have been fully trained before cleaning food slicers

Do this

● Check which cleaning chemicals are used in your kitchen. Read their instructions.
● Note where they are stored.
● Find out what protective clothing/equipment, if any, you need to use when applying each product.
● Check which items of equipment in your kitchen are listed on the *Prescribed Dangerous Machines Order 1964*.
● Read the safety notices beside or on the machines. If you cannot find any, report this to your supervisor.

PRECAUTIONS WHEN USING CLEANING CHEMICALS

● Always read and follow the instructions carefully. Pay attention to first aid procedures.
● Use protective clothing eg. gloves, when handling and using chemicals as some products are highly dangerous when in direct contact with human tissue. Refer to the COSHH regulations (*Control of Substances Hazardous to Health*). Ask your supervisor to supply you with this information.

● Ensure that you use the correct product for the appropriate job, eg. do not use chlorine bleach on food contact surfaces because it will taint and may contaminate the food.
● Always keep cleaning products in their own containers and make sure they are clearly labelled. Store them in a place which is not used for food storage.
● Never put cleaning chemicals into a food container or food into a chemical container.
● It is dangerous to mix cleaning chemicals. They may react and give off toxic fumes or they may become ineffective.
● If chemical cleaners require diluting, only do so immediately prior to use; otherwise they may lose their active qualities and become stagnant solutions which may harbour bacteria.
● Always use the correct concentration: if you do not dilute chemical cleaners enough the liquid may be difficult to rinse off and will lead to food contamination; if you dilute them too much they will be ineffective.
● Do not dispose of cleaning solutions in food preparation sinks.
● Clean the cleaning equipment itself (eg. brushes and cloths) after use. Store them away from food in a well-ventilated area to allow them to dry.

CLEANING CUTTING EQUIPMENT

Always refer to the operating manual for the specific details of how to clean the cutting equipment that you use in your kitchen. As a general rule, follow the steps given here.

1 When you have finished using the machine, *switch it off and remove the plug from the wall socket*. If it is connected directly to a mains unit, isolate it by switching off the electricity supply to the machine.
  ● It is important to isolate the equipment fully so that there is no danger of it being accidentally switched on either when the blades are exposed, or when the machine has not been assembled correctly. This could cause serious injury and/or damage to the machine.
  ● When cleaning the equipment you will be using plenty of water and if the machine is still connected to the mains there is risk of an electric shock.

> **MEMORY JOGGER**
>
> Why should you turn off and dismantle cutting equipment before cleaning?

Always unplug a mincing machine before cleaning

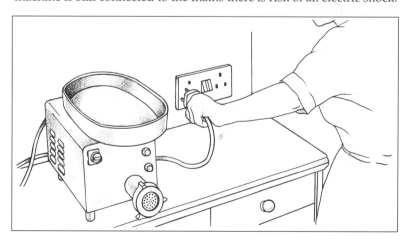

2 Carefully remove the guards and any removable parts. eg. blades, etc.
3 Wash the individual parts in hot detergent water, and dry. *Never leave machinery parts in a sink*.
4 Clean the machine itself, taking care not to use excessive water around the electrical connections.
5 Wash the cutting blades very carefully, using a brush.
6 Check any inside corners for food debris that may have collected.
7 Thoroughly dry the machine and any separate parts.

8 Reassemble the machine. Make sure that all parts fit correctly and securely.
9 Dry your hands and reconnect the machine to the mains. Switch it on to check that it is functioning correctly.
10 Disconnect from the mains until required.

Essential knowledge	Equipment must be turned off and dismantled before cleaning in order to: ● ensure that parts are cleaned correctly ● prevent injury to the person cleaning ● prevent damage to equipment ● conserve energy.

Points to note when cleaning cutting machines

● Hand-held cutting utensils such as mandolins need to be carefully cleaned with hot detergent water. Use a brush to clean the blade, then rinse clean and dry carefully. Never leave any blades or cutting instruments in a sink.
● Accidents with cutting equipment are caused by carelessness and lack of concentration. In the event of an accident, report it to your supervisor and the on-site first aider immediately (see Unit NG1: *Maintaining a safe and secure working environment* pages 22–25). Apply emergency first aid if you have been trained.

Do this	● Make a list of the cutting equipment in your kitchen. ● If you are aged over 18, ask for training in using, dismantling, cleaning and reassembling the cutting equipment in your kitchen. ● Once you have been trained, clean the cutting equipment in your kitchen. ● Make a note of how to contact your on-site first aider.

Case study	*You are asked to finish washing up the utensils and equipment after service. The sink is full of hot soapy water, you put your hand in to check what is already in there and feel a searing pain. You pull your hand out of the water and see a deep cut across the palm of your hand. The blade from a slicing machine was left in the sink.* *1 What are the rules for cleaning cutting equipment?* *2 Who is responsible for safety in the kitchen?* *3 What needs to happen as a result of this incident?*

What have you learned	1 List four reasons why we clean cutting equipment. 2 Why must equipment be turned off and dismantled before cleaning? 3 Why is it important to plan the time to clean? 4 What do you need to check before using a cleaning chemical? 5 Which machines are listed in the *Prescribed Dangerous Machines Order 1964*? 6 State five precautions to observe when cleaning cutting equipment. 7 What should you do in the event of an accident? 8 Which utensils should never be left in a sink?

ELEMENT 2: Maintain cutting equipment

PROFESSIONAL CUTTING EQUIPMENT

The types of cutting equipment in used in professional kitchens is very different to the smaller domestic versions that you may have used at home. They are designed for heavy duty work in a busy environment and are very expensive.

Most businesses will have a maintenance contract for the large equipment, and this can also be very expensive. It is therefore very important that you know how to use and maintain these valuable assets.

As mentioned in the previous element you must not operate cutting equipment if you have not been properly trained and if you are under 18 you may not dismantle or clean it.

Points to note when maintaining cutting equipment

Always ensure that the equipment is positioned in the correct area and that it is stable. Rotary type cutting equipment will vibrate when in use and it is important that you keep an eye on it to check that it is stable.

Read the manufacturer's instructions to learn the best practice for storage and use.

Large cutting equipment is often very heavy (to keep it stable) and you may need help if you have to move it. Check the weight before you attempt to lift it and get help from a colleague if necessary. It is easy to strain your back if you lift equipment incorrectly. Always keep your head up and your back straight (see Unit NG1: *Maintain a safe environment* pages 25–26). Ensure that the equipment is isolated and the blades are secure before moving it.

Cutting equipment is extremely dangerous and can cause serious accidents if it is not in correct working order. Under the *Health and Safety at Work Act (1974)*, you have a legal responsibility to ensure that you take reasonable care of yourself and others at work.

Always check the equipment regularly; if you notice that a piece of equipment is faulty or has no safety guard, report it to your supervisor immediately. Place a clear sign or notice warning others not to use it and make sure that the equipment is isolated by removing the plug from the socket or switching off its electricity supply.

MEMORY JOGGER

What are the precautions you need to take when lifting cutting equipment?

MEMORY JOGGER

What do you need to do if you notice a fault with a piece of equipment?

Do this

- Ask your supervisor for the manufacturer's instructions for the equipment you have to use and read it.
- Find out how much each piece of cutting equipment in your area costs when brand new.
- How much does it cost to have cutting equipment repaired? For example: call out charge, new blade(s), new motor, new bowl.
- Does your work place have a contract for the maintenance of the cutting equipment?
- Find out how much the contract costs.

Case study

You go to use the gravity feed slicer and when you switch it on it makes the terrible sound of metal scraping metal and then stops. You also notice the smell of burning grease from the back of the slicer.

1   What may have happened?
2   How could this have been caused?
3   What can you do to ensure this never happens again?

What have you learned

1   Why is it important to know and follow the manufacturer's procedures for operation, cleaning and maintenance of a machine?
2   How should you lift cutting equipment?
3   What do you need to do if you discover a fault with a piece of equipment?
4   How can you prevent accidents with cutting equipment?
5   What are your responsibilities under the Health and Safety at Work Act?

Get ahead

1   Research the cases of food poisoning known to have been caused by unhygienic cutting equipment.
2   List the chemical names of substances present in some cleaning agents that may damage cutting equipment.
3   Read through the training guidance notes for all of the dangerous equipment in your workplace.

Unit 2ND22

Maintain and promote hygiene in food storage, preparation and cooking

This chapter covers:

ELEMENT 1: **Maintain and promote food hygiene in food storage**

ELEMENT 2: **Maintain and promote hygiene in food preparation and cooking**

What you need to do

- Ensure that you always maintain a very high standard of personal hygiene.
- Check that your work areas and equipment are both clean and hygienic.
- Check that all food items are in good hygienic condition when they are delivered.
- See that all food items are stored correctly.
- Use food items in the correct rotation.

- Use separate equipment for preparing raw and high risk food items.
- Ensure that all food items are kept at a safe temperature during cooking.
- Identify and report any problems regarding food hygiene to your supervisor.
- Check that waste bins are kept covered and away from food.
- Work in an organised and efficient manner in line with the organisational procedures and legal requirements.

What you need to know

- How to store all food items safely.
- Why all storage areas and equipment must be kept hygienic.
- How to lift heavy items correctly.
- What the main threats of contamination are.
- How to identify food pest infestation.
- Why time and temperature are so important when storing and cooking food.
- Why it is essential to have high standards of personal hygiene.

- How to check if food deliveries are in good hygienic condition before accepting delivery.
- How to identify unfit food and how to dispose of it correctly.
- Why raw and cooked food should be stored separately.
- What cross-contamination is and how to prevent it.
- How to defrost food items in a hygienic way.
- What your responsibilities are under the food hygiene regulations.

INTRODUCTION

Over the past 10 years there has been an four-fold increase in the reported cases of food poisoning. (See Chart on p. 98.) And this is only the tip of the iceberg: it is recognised that only 1 in 10 people who suffer the symptoms of food poisoning actually report it. So there are at present an estimated 825,000 cases of food poisoning in the UK every year!

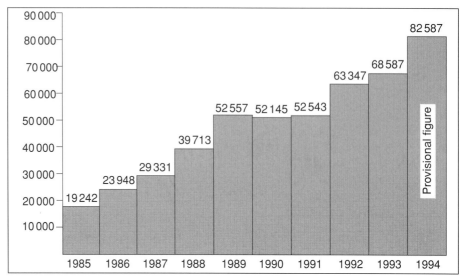

Reported cases of food poisoning

Source: *Office of Population Censuses and Surveys*

If your body cannot retain any liquids because you are constantly vomiting and have diarrhoea you will quickly become very weak. In fact these symptoms can even cause death in the very young, the very old and those already ill.

You do not want to be responsible for causing the pain and discomfort of persistent vomiting and diarrhoea or even the death of another person, so maintaining and promoting high standards of food hygiene is an essential role of any food handler.

You are also legally bound to adhere to the food safety requirements outlined in the *Food Safety Act 1990*, and the *General Food Hygiene Regulations 1995* (see Unit NG1 pages 2–3).

Remember: As a food handler you have a legal and moral responsibility to practise the highest standards of food hygiene.

There is a lot of information in this book about the sources of food poisoning and personal hygiene. See for example Unit NG1 page 4. The safe and hygienic storage of food items is detailed in Unit 2ND11 pages 65–89. You will also find notes on the safe and hygienic cleaning of food production areas, equipment and utensils in Unit 1ND1 pages 47–55.

If you want to be able to promote and maintain good standards of hygiene it is important to understand the main causes of food poisoning and how to protect food from contamination.

The most common cause of food poisoning is from *bacteria* which we can't see – millions would fit on a pinhead. They are found everywhere, but in such small numbers that they don't cause any harm.

It is important to note that not all bacteria are harmful, some are even essential for our good health!

Essential knowledge	**Sources of bacteria:**	
	1 humans	6 raw vegetables
	2 insects	7 dust and dirt
	3 animals	8 untreated water
	4 raw meat	9 refuse and rubbish
	5 fish and poultry	10 sewage

There are basically three types of bacteria:
● Useful: To make special food items like cheese, yoghurt, vinegars etc.
● Spoilage: These cause food to go off and can be identified by smell, taste, sight and touch.
● Pathogenic: These cause serious illness and do not change the appearance of the food when they are present, so they are very difficult to identify (this can only be done in a laboratory).

The bacteria that cause poisoning are called *pathogens*. The most common pathogenic bacteria are *Salmonella*, *Clostridium Perfrigens* and *Staphylococcus Aureus*. They can only be detected in a laboratory and they do not usually affect the taste, smell or look of the food.

Salmonella
Sources: raw meat, eggs, poultry, animals, sewage.
Onset time: 6–72 hours.
Symptoms: abdominal pains, diarrhoea, fever, vomiting, dehydration.
Special characteristics: There are over 200 different types of *salmonella* some need only very few bacteria to cause serious illness.

Clostridium Perfrigens
Sources: raw meat, soil, excreta, insects.
Onset time: 8–22 hours.
Symptoms: abdominal pain, diarrhoea.
Special characteristics: produces a spore which protects the bacteria from high temperatures (spores may even survive hours of boiling).

Staphylococcus Aureus
Sources: skin, nose, boils, cuts, raw milk.
Onset time: 1–6 hours.
Symptoms: vomiting, abdominal pains, lower-than-normal temperatures.
Special characteristics: produces a toxin which is not destroyed by heat.

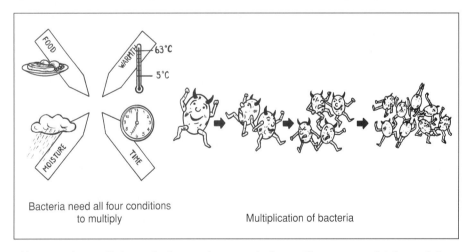

Bacteria need all four conditions to multiply

Multiplication of bacteria

How bacteria multiply

MEMORY JOGGER

What are high risk foods?
Give five examples

If bacteria have all the right factors for growth they will start to multiply, and then you may very soon have a serious problem.

The way bacteria grow is by splitting in two every 10–20 minutes. In the right conditions a single bacteria can easily multiply to 100,000,000 in eight or nine hours!

High risk food
This is food that will help bacteria to grow more quickly. It is usually moist and high in protein eg. cooked meat, fish and shellfish, eggs, dairy produce (milk, cream) soups, sauces, stocks, cooked rice.

Moisture
This is found in most food, in the air, and in poorly ventilated storage areas.

Warmth
The right temperature for bacteria to grow most quickly is about the same as our body temperature, 37 °C (99 °F). Room temperature is also ideal. There is a temperature range called the *danger zone*: when any food is in this zone there is a high risk of any bacteria present multiplying. This zone is between 5°C and 63°C (41°F and 145°F). Food items should never be left lying around in the danger zone.

Time
The bacteria need time to grow so you must ensure that food items are in the danger zone for the minimum amount of time.

MEMORY JOGGER

What is the temperature range of the danger zone?

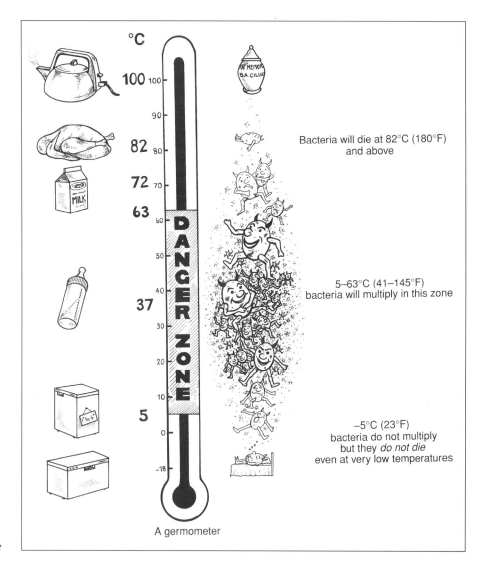

A germometer

Bacteria will die at 82°C (180°F) and above

5–63°C (41–145°F) bacteria will multiply in this zone

–5°C (23°F) bacteria do not multiply but they *do not die* even at very low temperatures

Keep out of the danger zone

Essential knowledge	Bacteria need four factors to grow: food moisture warmth time
	● Always store food out of the *danger zone* which is 5–63 °C (41–145 °F).
	● Ensure that when preparing food items, you keep the time that the food is in the danger zone to a minimum.

CONTAMINATION

This is basically anything in food that should not be there!

There are different kinds of contamination, for example:
- *Bacterial contamination*: from food pests, poor personal hygiene, poor storage and poor working practices.
- *Cross-contamination*: where the bacteria from a source like raw meat comes in contact with high risk food, either directly by touching or indirectly via a dirty knife or poorly cleaned chopping board.
- *Physical contamination*: where hair, plasters, insects, wood, glass, etc. fall into the food.
- *Chemical contamination*: where food preparation surfaces or equipment have not been rinsed properly after cleaning, or cleaning chemicals are stored with food items or in food containers. You can also get chemical contamination from pesticides on unwashed fruit and vegetables.

> **MEMORY JOGGER**
>
> What is cross-contamination?

YOUR RESPONSIBILITY

Maintaining high standards of hygiene in your work and storage areas will deny food poisoning bacteria the conditions they need to grow and multiply.

There is now a legal requirement placed upon **all people** who handle food in any way to be responsible for using hygienic working practices.

This begins with being clean. In the same way that doctors scrub up before an operation and only use sterile equipment, chefs must do the same by making sure that they keep themselves and the equipment they use as clean as possible.

Always check deliveries for any signs of contamination or damage from food pests (see opposite) and report any problems immediately to your supervisor.

THE TEN MOST COMMON CAUSES OF FOOD POISONING

In a report written by a working party looking into the causes of food poisoning, a list of the ten most common causes was given:

> **MEMORY JOGGER**
>
> The party food looks good, smells good, even tastes good! Why might it be poisonous?

1 Food is prepared too far in advance
Preparing food in advance is necessary for good kitchen organisation but great care needs to be taken with handling and storage, otherwise the food poisoning bacteria will have enough time to grow and multiply. Always use food items and stores in the correct rotation; first-in, first-out.

2 Food stored at room temperature
Warmth is one of the key conditions needed for bacteria to grow. As kitchens are warm places, if food is left out for any length of time the bacteria will multiply rapidly and contaminate the food.

3 Cooling food too slowly before refrigerating it
Never put hot food directly into a refrigerator or cold room. Cool the food down first by spreading it out on trays or cooling containers in a sink of iced water. The sooner the food is cold, the less chance there is of it becoming contaminated. Cooling time should not be more than $1\frac{1}{2}$ hours.

4 Not reheating food enough to kill food poisoning bacteria
All food which has been cooked and then cooled for storage is a potential risk. It is possible for any bacteria present to multiply during the cooling process and if the food is not reheated properly the bacteria will continue to grow until the food is eaten. Always make sure that reheated food is thoroughly hot (70 °C/165 °F) throughout for at least two minutes, as this is the only way to guarantee its safety.

5 Using food contaminated with bacteria

The best way to make sure that food remains safe is to practise very high standards of food hygiene. Ensure that there is no risk of cross-contamination from raw meat, dirty equipment, bad personal habits or unwashed hands. Always dispose of leftovers and waste in a covered bin and then wash your hands.

6 Under-cooking meat and poultry

All raw meat and poultry contain bacteria and it is therefor essential to make sure that these bacteria are killed by sufficient cooking. Pork and poultry should always be cooked until they are 'well done'.

7 Not thawing frozen meat and poultry properly

It is very dangerous to try to cook meat or poultry which is still frozen inside. All the heat used to cook the food will be spent thawing the meat out. This can result in the food looking as if it is ready, or even overdone, on the outside, but on the inside it could still be raw, leaving any bacteria present to multiply and contaminate the food. (See Unit 2ND11 pages 84–86 for the correct procedures for defrosting.)

8 Cooked foods cross-contaminated by raw foods

All raw and cooked foods must be completely covered when stored to avoid cross-contamination. Any bacteria from a raw piece of meat or poultry may remain on a knife or chopping board if these are not thoroughly washed.

So remember to *clean as you go* and to wash your hands frequently especially after you handle raw foods, rubbish or after taking a break.

9 Storing hot foods below 63 °C (145 °F) and cold foods above 5 °C(41 °F)

Bacteria cannot multiply below 5°C (41 °F) or above 63 °C (145 °F). Anything within this temperature band is in the *danger zone*. All fridges and hot storage areas need to be regularly checked to make sure that the food stored remains outside this zone.

10 Infected food handlers

If you become ill, it is against the law for you to handle food. There is a high risk that you will contaminate the food and cause other people to become ill. Always report any illness to your head chef and if you suspect food poisoning, check with your doctor. You will need a doctor's certificate to be able to return to work.

PEST CONTROL

Food pests are any animals, birds or insects which live on food.

There a number of ways in which they contaminate food:
- eating food and spreading bacteria from their feet and saliva as they eat
- droppings
- urinating on food
- carrying bacteria on their bodies
- physical contamination (hairs, dead bodies etc.).

Examples of food pests are:
Insects: cockroaches, flies, ants, silverfish, wasps
Rodents: rats and mice
Domestic pets: cats and dogs
Birds: pigeons, sparrows, starlings

As a food handler it is important to be able to identify the signs of infestation, these include:
rodents: gnaw marks, spillages, damage to food stocks, droppings and visual sighting
insects: visual sightings, eggs, larvae and maggots.

Always report any signs of infestation immediately to your supervisor.

Larder beetle

Grain weevil

Silverfish

Rust red flour beetle

Feral pigeon

House mouse

Brown rat

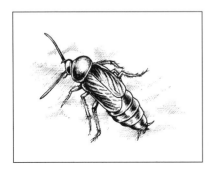

Cockroach

House flies

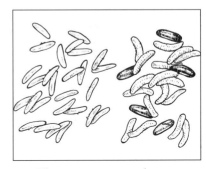

Fly eggs, maggots and pupae

Never try and deal with the problem by yourself because you may cause more harm by not setting the right sort of traps or using poisons incorrectly. Your local authority will give advice on what to do.

You can limit pests by ensuring that you:
● keep all bins covered and dispose of waste correctly
● keep your work areas clean and well lit
● do not leave food lying about, see that all food is stored off the floor and in vermin-proof containers
● ensure windows have screens; all holes and cracks should be reported.

If you discover any damage to food or food storage containers report it to your supervisor immediately. All of the contaminated food must be discarded and the surrounding area thoroughly cleaned and disinfected.

<table>
<tr>
<td>

Essential knowledge

</td>
<td>

Always report any signs of infestation to your supervisor immediately.
Food pests will contaminate food by:
- eating food and spreading bacteria from their feet and saliva as they eat
- droppings
- urinating on food
- carrying bacteria on their bodies
- physical contamination (hairs, dead bodies etc.)

</td>
</tr>
</table>

THE LAWS REGARDING FOOD HYGIENE

There are two main laws regarding food hygiene and they are concerned with the production, preparation and sale of food. The purpose of these laws is to prevent outbreaks of food poisoning and the sale of unfit food to the public.

The Food Safety Act 1990

This is a wide-ranging law which updated the previous laws and affects everyone working in the production, processing, storage, distribution and sale of food.

The aim of this law is:
- to ensure that all food for sale is safe to eat and not presented in a misleading way
- to strengthen legal powers and penalties
- to keep in line with the rest of the European Union
- to keep pace with technology.

The main offences under the act are:
- selling or being in possession of food which does not meet the *food safety requirements*
- producing food that is injurious to health
- selling food which is not of the *nature, substance* or *quality* demanded by the person buying it
- falsely describing, or presenting food in a misleading way.

The food safety requirements are that it must not be rendered injurious to health, for example become contaminated either through neglect or intentionally tampering with the food, so that it would be unreasonable to expect it to be eaten. The food would be considered unfit if it was, for example, spoilt, rotten or contained a dead mouse.

It is an offence to make food harmful even if the person responsible did not know that this would be the result eg. inadequately reheating food which results in it being unfit for consumption.

Food that is 'not of the nature, substance or quality' would, for example, mean selling haddock in batter and calling it cod, serving a meat stew with too little meat (and too much fat) in it, skimmed milk with too much fat, or serving sour cream on fresh cream buns.

For most offences the crown courts will be able to send offenders to prison for up to two years and/or impose an unlimited fine. A magistrates court can set fines for up to £20,000 per offence.

The General Food Hygiene Regulations 1995

The aim of these regulations is to make sure that all the countries in the European Community have the same rules regarding food hygiene. Anyone who cleans utensils or equipment which come in contact with food or anyone who handles food and could affect its safety must follow the regulations.

The regulations include the basic requirements for food businesses, they should:
- be clean and in good condition
- be designed and constructed so that they are easy to clean and will keep pests away
- have a good supply of drinking water
- have satisfactory lighting and ventilation
- provide toilets that do not lead directly into food rooms
- have adequate hand washing facilities
- have adequate drainage and refuse collection.

Personal hygiene for food handlers

All staff working with food need to maintain a very high standard of personal cleanliness. This includes clean and where appropriate, protective over-clothing.

You should:
- observe good personal hygiene
- wash your hands regularly when handling food
- never smoke in food preparation, storage or service areas
- report any illness to your supervisor immediately. For example; infected wounds, skin or ear infections, vomiting or diarrhoea.

Case study

While filleting some fish you accidentally pricked your finger on a fish-bone. It's only a tiny nick with hardly a speck of blood, you wipe your hand and carry on. The next day you notice a throbbing in your finger but the nick from the day before looks healed over so you carry on.

That evening at work there are three telephone calls from guests to the restaurant manager claiming food poisoning. They all said they had been vomiting a few hours after lunch.

1   What is the bacteria that would have caused the poisoning?
2   What needs to be done to prevent such an incident?
3   Who is responsible in this case?

Prevention of contamination

It is very important for all people who work with food to take every precaution to prevent the food from becoming contaminated. This has been outlined on previous pages. *See pages 101–103.*

Training and supervision of food handlers

All staff need to be given adequate instruction and/or training to ensure that they are aware of the risks and their responsibilities regarding food hygiene.

Supplies of raw materials

All deliveries need to be checked and any material which you suspect may cause food to be harmful eg. subject to contamination or infestation, must be rejected.

The people who check up on food premises are called Environmental Health Officers (EHOs). They have the similar powers to police officers and can enter any food premises without a search warrant. They can inspect food and any records to see that they are in order. They can seize food and ask for it to be condemned. They must also be given assistance and truthful answers to their questions.

If a food premises fails to meet the requirements of the law the Environmental Health Officer will issue an *Improvement Notice*. This outlines what the owner must do to put things right and gives the time by which it must be done.

If a business is convicted by a court and it is felt that there is a risk to the public, a prohibition order will be issued to close all or part of the premises.

If the officer believes that the business poses an imminent risk to the health of the public he or she may close it down with an *Emergency prohibition notice*. The case would then be brought to court.

If a court concludes that a business poses an imminent risk to public health it will issue an *Emergency prohibition order* to close the business down.

ELEMENT 1: Maintain and promote food hygiene in food storage

YOUR BODY

You have a legal and moral responsibility to practice high standards of hygiene. Humans are a major source of bacteria so you will need to keep your body and clothing clean. Maintaining clean hands is also critical.

Always wash your hands:
● before starting work
● before handling food
● after handling raw meat and when changing tasks
● after visiting the toilet or handling rubbish/waste
● after touching you nose, ears or hair
● after coughing, sneezing or smoking.

As a food handler it is also important to be aware of bad habits which are unhygienic.

Always avoid:
● licking fingers when separating sheets of paper
● picking, scratching or touching you nose
● scratching your head or picking spots
● tasting food with your fingers or an unwashed spoon
● coughing or sneezing near or over food
● smoking
● using hand wash basins for washing food utensil.

(See Unit NG1 pages 4–8 for more information.)

YOUR WORKING AREA

Remember to 'clean as you go'! It is easiest to wash down and clean equipment immediately after use. Ensure that you use the correct chemicals and rinse down well to avoid contamination. (See Unit 1ND1 page 50 for specific information relating to cleaning your work area.)

DELIVERY OF FOOD ITEMS

Your own standards of hygiene may be good but if the food you buy is not up to standard, you may be held responsible if you accept food deliveries which fall below the required standard. Always check with your supervisor that you are fully trained to know the minimum standards that you require. You will need to know the specifications of fish and meat, the temperature of frozen and chilled foods, and the standards for dried and canned foods.

● Food that needs to be refrigerated should not be accepted if the temperature is above 10 °C (50 °F) because any bacteria present may be multiplying and contaminating it.

● Any frozen food delivered at a temperature higher than −12 °C (10 °F) should also be rejected.

(The key points in accepting deliveries of different food types are in Unit 2ND11 pages 65–82.)

FOOD STORAGE

<table>
<tr><td>**MEMORY JOGGER**</td></tr>
<tr><td>What is the correct temperature for the following: freezer, fridge, hot cupboard?</td></tr>
</table>

When storing food items always keep them covered and ensure that they are stored at the correct temperature. All raw foods must be stored separate from cooked food to prevent cross-contamination. If it is not possible to use separate fridges always place raw food below cooked food.

To ensure that stored food remains safe the temperature must be checked regularly:

Freezers	−18 °C (0 °F)	All deep frozen foods
Fridges	1–4 °C (34–39 °F)	All high risk foods eg. meat. poultry, fish, dairy, eggs
Dry store	10–15 °C (50–59 °F)	All dried, canned and some preserved foods
Hot storage	70–75 °C (165–174 °F)	All cooked food ready for service

(For more details on the various types of food items and their storage see Unit 2ND11 pages 65–89.)

STOCK ROTATION

To ensure that the stored food is maintained in the best possible condition it is essential to rotate stock. Whatever goes in first must come out first. Always place the new stock at the back so that the old food comes to the front and is used first.

● Check sell-by and best-before dates (It is against the law to have out-of-date stock in your stores.).

● Only order what you need to prevent the unnecessary storage of perishable foods.

● Prolonged storage can lead to mould and possible infestation of food pests.

● If you notice that any food is stored incorrectly or has become unfit, report it to your supervisor.

Do this

● Re-read Unit NG1 Element 1: *Maintain personal health and hygiene* and Unit 2ND11 *Receive, handle and store food deliveries*

● Check the temperature records for the cold storage areas in your workplace. Is the temperature correct?

● Find out what precautions are taken in your work area to prevent pest infestation.

● Do some spot checks on the temperatures of frozen food deliveries; report the results to you supervisor.

● Do some spot checks of temperature of the food stored in the hot cupboard; report the results to you supervisor.

● Identify any potential hygiene hazards in your work areas make suggestions to improve them to your supervisor.

What have you learned

1 What do bacteria need to multiply?
2 What is the *danger zone*?
3 What are the three most common pathogenic bacteria?
4 How do pests contaminate food?
5 List what do you can do to protect food from contamination?
6 What are your responsibilities under the food laws?
7 What are the aims of the food laws?
8 Who checks if businesses are complying with the law and what powers do they have?

ELEMENT 2:   Maintain and promote hygiene in food preparation and cooking

PERSONAL HYGIENE

We have already discussed the importance of personal hygiene and why you need to keep your body and especially your hands clean. (See Unit NG1 pages 2–8.)

YOUR WORKING AREA

When preparing and cooking food you must also check that the cooking areas and equipment are in a clean condition. Many cases of food poisoning are due to poor standards of hygiene in these areas. Always clean down immediately after service or after using a particular piece of equipment. Take great care, when using strong cleaning chemicals, that you rinse down well so that there are no chemical residues which may contaminate food that is being cooked.

When preparing raw and high risk food items it is important to use separate equipment. This prevents the possible cross-contamination from the bacteria present in the raw food. Chopping boards, knives and containers need to be cleaned and disinfected after contact with raw food. You can use a sanitiser to save time. A sanitiser will clean and disinfect at the same time. Another way to disinfect is to rinse equipment in very hot water (minimum 82 °C/179 °F). (See Unit 1ND1 pages 47–55, for more details.)

MEMORY JOGGER

What is the risk of using the same equipment for raw and cooked foods?

UNFIT FOOD AND WASTE

If you discover that any food item is unfit by sight, smell, taste or touch you must report it to your supervisor and dispose of it safely. Make sure that the unfit food is discarded in a waste disposal unit or in a covered waste bin. It is also important to thoroughly wash your hands and ensure that any cloths or aprons that may have been soiled are changed afterwards.

Waste bins need to be changed regularly and should never be allowed to become too full as this attracts pests and bad odours. It also makes them difficult to move and empty.

Always follow these guidelines
● Waste bins, their lids and surrounding areas must be thoroughly cleaned and disinfected.
● Store waste in the correct designated areas. These should be away from food preparation and cooking areas, corridors and fire exits.

MEMORY JOGGER

Why do you need to dispose of waste correctly?

TEMPERATURE CONTROL

If food is within the danger zone (5–63 °C/41–145 °F) any bacteria present will start to multiply. It is therefore essential to keep the preparation time of food in this zone to an absolute minimum. When cooking food you must monitor the temperature to ensure that it stays hot enough. This is important if you want to complete the cooking on time. There is also a risk that if the temperature does not exceed 63 °C (145 °F) that some bacteria may survive and this could lead to serious contamination.

Remember: **When re-heating food items it is critical to ensure that the temperature is a minimum of 70 °C (165 °F) throughout for at least two minutes.**

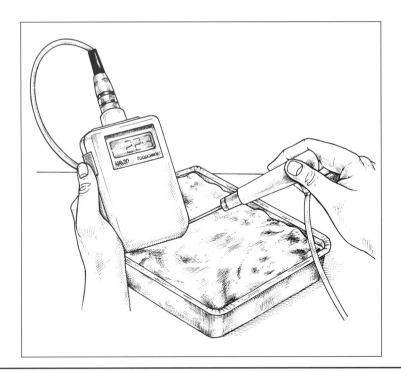

Make sure that heat-and-serve-food is re-heated correctly, according to the instructions. Never cook it for less than the recommended time

Case study

The chef asks you to defrost a turkey for the special party next day. You place it in the fridge to thaw out. The next day you cook the turkey carefully, checking the cooking time for the weight of the bird and the cooking temperature. After the stipulated time the turkey looks perfect and is sent to the carvery to be served to the special party. During the next three days there are a number of calls claiming food poisoning.
1 *Which bacteria do you think may have caused the poisoning?*
2 *What is the likely cause of the outbreak?*
3 *What checks need to be made to prevent this happening?*
4 *What may happen as a result of this incident?*

Do this

- Check the temperature of food being prepared in the kitchen. Is the temperature correct? How long has it been at this temperature?
- Find out what the correct cooking times and temperatures are for beef, pork and turkey.
- Identify any potential hygiene hazards in your preparation and cooking areas. Make suggestions to improve them to your supervisor.

What have you learned

1 What are the hygiene risks when preparing food?
2 What temperature does water need to be at to disinfect?
3 How should you dispose of unfit food?
4 What are the risks of re-heating food?
5 What are your responsibilities under the food laws?

Get ahead

1 Call the local Department of Health and ask for more information of the *Food Safety Act 1990* and *The General Food Hygiene Regulations 1995*.
2 Call your local newspaper and ask which local food premises have been prosecuted recently for breaking the food laws and what offences they committed.
3 Call your local authority and ask for more information on food pests.
4 Visit different food production businesses, eg. a slaughterhouse, a cook-chill/vacuum packing business, a bakery and a food manufacturer to compare their hygiene standards.

Index

Page references in italics indicate illustrations